A WHITE HOUSE GARDEN COOKBOOK

HEALTHY IDEAS FROM THE First Family FOR Your Family

Clara Silverstein

RED ROCK PRESS   NEW YORK, NEW YORK

A White House Garden Cookbook

ISBN 978-1933176-35-2

Red Rock Press
New York, New York

www.RedRockPress.com

This book is an independent journalistic project, not sponsored by the White House or any other party.

Cover and title-page garden photos by Joyce N. Boghosian, The White House
    Blog/Creative Common Licence
Cover Oval photo, courtesy of Boise Urban Garden School
Original interior drawings by Miki Harder
Index by Sayre Van Young

Design by Susan Smilanic, Studio 21, Durango CO

Library of Congress Cataloging-in-Publication Data

Silverstein, Clara, 1960-
  The White House Garden cookbook : healthy ideas from the first family
for your family / Clara Silverstein.
      p. cm.
  Includes bibliographical references and index.
  ISBN 978-1-933176-35-2
1. Cookery (Vegetables) 2. Cookery, American. 3. White House Gardens
(Washington, D.C.)—Pictorial works. 4. Vegetable gardening—United
States. 5. Heirloom varieties (Plants)—United States. 6. Obama,
Michelle, 1964- I. Title.
  TX801.S57178 2010
  641.59753—dc22
                              2010004579

Printed in Canada

Cover Oval: Young cooks are Kira Jenkins, Isabel Foxcroft, Nick, Harrison Clement of Boise [Idaho] Urban Garden School (BUGS).

TABLE OF CONTENTS

**For my children,
Jordan and Martha**

Introduction

There's an amazing change going on in American backyards, schoolyards and community parks. It's slow and sometimes faltering, fueled mostly by sunshine and rain. Dump-truck loads of manure, blistered hands and, most especially, cheerful chatter are part of the mix.

The White House Kitchen Garden has inspired home and community gardeners. When Michelle Obama broke ground in the spring of 2009, she faced the challenge of creating a brand new garden where nothing but grass grew. The last time a First Lady had planted a garden was 1943, when Eleanor Roosevelt's modest Victory Garden promoted can-do patriotism at the height of World War II.

Across America there are family and community gardeners who dug their spades into the good earth and spent kitchen time bringing fresh flavors to the table, absent a White House signal but perhaps influenced by contemporary fresh-food pioneers such as Alice Waters of Berkeley, California. But what happens in Washington D.C. doesn't stay there. A new administration's ideas can energize the like-minded across the globe and spark new enthusiasts from sea to shining sea.

Still, a garden is dirty work. Brown transforms to green, although sometimes the starting line is soggy, and the first steps require chunking up and enriching long-ignored potential soil. From the barrenness, spots of green will emerge and colors will expand to red, purple, orange and yellow.

These new rainbows in the ground are the vegetable gardens planted, tended and harvested largely by families

and, in some programs, children. Enthusiasm for them seems to be spreading as fast as a patch of mint.

Mrs. Obama has made healthy eating for children an important part of her message about the garden since she lifted the first shovel of dirt. Being a mom gives her a special interest in this area. "The whole point of this garden," she explained at the groundbreaking, "is that I want to make sure that our family, as well as the staff and all the people who come to the White House and eat our food, get access to really fresh vegetables and fruits." A first-ever White House beehive puts honey on the table, too.

Helping her that day and several times during the garden's first season were fifth graders from the Bancroft School in Washington, D.C. Mrs. Obama let them in on one of the ways that she coaxes her daughters to try new foods. "If they were involved in planting and picking it, they were much more curious about giving it a try," she said.

Great ideas have no single owners, and a White House garden is no exception. Its roots reach back to the early 19th-century kitchen gardens, which were organic because everything was back then. John Adams, the first president to reside at the White House (the building was not yet finished when George Washington held office), was also the first to request a vegetable patch. Unfortunately, it was not finished until 1801, after Abigail and John Adams had moved out.

Adams' successor, Thomas Jefferson, was an avid

Joyce N. Boghosian/White House Blog/Common Copyright

5

gardener. The current White House garden contains seeds and sprouts descended from his garden at Monticello.

Dolly Madison sent up bushels of homegrown Virginia strawberries for her husband James' inaugural celebration. The berries were used to flavor and color a then-unique dessert created by Sallie Shadd, a freed slave whose family ran a tearoom in Delaware. The inaugural treat was strawberry ice cream.

The ambitious new White House Kitchen Garden is the first full-scale vegetable garden at the White House since Theodore and Edith Roosevelt lived there in 1902, back when the United States was still a nation of farmers.

The creating of this cookbook seemed a good occasion to look at some recipes of former First Families and adapt them for families today. Most of the included White House recipes, however, are recent.

It takes a far-flung nation to come together not only with its home-grown fruits, vegetables and herbs, but also with its favorite tastes.

I checked in with community gardening groups around the nation to find out what they are making with all the food that they harvest, with an emphasis on groups where families or kids participate in the cooking. I wanted plenty of kid-certified recipes in this collection to dispel the notion that kids don't like and won't eat vegetables. Young gardeners, from teenagers to preschoolers, report that they pick and eat vegetables right on the spot, even unexpected ones, such as okra. When I asked for recipes, garden-group leaders and kids enthusiastically responded, even if their access to a kitchen and equipment was limited to a blender plugged into an outlet at the gardening shed.

We are sharing some of the best with you, as well as a few other seasonal recipes that we developed ourselves. Everything that we use in the book contains at least one ingredient that matches something grown at the White House. All the recipes in this collection have been chosen with a view to family use and enjoyment of them. Since they came from so many different sources, I rewrote and adapted many of them to fit the book's format, without changing the basic concepts. I also tested and modernized recipes from early presidents. The family that cooks together experiences time-tested pleasures. More than one cook can stir the pot, although no recipe requires this.

A few recipes include meat, either to reflect the offerings at White House family or official meals, or dishes being prepared by some garden groups around the country. Not everyone lives by corn and cranberries alone, but whether as centerpiece contributions or side dishes, the crispy or colorful preparations of locally-grown vegetables and fruits are the stars of this book.

We invite you to try the recipes in this collection with produce that you grow yourself. If you don't have access to a garden or enough time to plant one, do the next best thing and visit a farmer's market or a local farm stand. A big, floppy bunch of lettuce might look like a lab experiment gone awry, and carrots might be covered with so much dirt that they look more brown than orange. Once you wash fresh produce, it will taste more flavorful than anything wrapped in plastic.

Good food nourishes both body and brain. You can take pride in what you are doing to ensure your family's well being. After all, the First Lady is doing it, too, though she probably doesn't have to wash the dishes.

—— Clara Silverstein
Boston, Massachusetts

PART I

A Time to Think

The best-planned gardens are mulled over, cultivated in the mind beforehand and sometimes painstakingly sketched on page (or screen), too. Michelle Obama's garden idea started in her kitchen long before she realized she would be First Lady. "Before I was here, I had a job and I was always rushing around, and the kids' schedules were busy," she told a group of children visiting the White House during Take Your Child to Work Day.

"You guys know that feeling, right? You come home, you're rushing, Mom's just gotten home from work. Or you're [the mom] and you're trying to figure out what you're going to feed your kids that is healthy, and you don't have time to prepare something. So you pop in something quick, and it's not always the best thing."

If Mrs. Obama sounded as if she'd been that harried mom, it's probably because she had been. Not long ago, she was a Chicago lawyer with two little girls and a husband working a thousand miles away –– as a U.S. senator. Michelle's own mother was also working outside the home back then.

Some people dream of a vegetable patch because they have a vision of sun-warmed soil sifting through their fingers and a row of vibrant tomatoes before them. Michelle Obama, perhaps, thought of the tomato part. Yet from the get-go, her notion of a garden was rooted in her desire to see her children eat better.

Long before her husband started his campaign for the presidency, Mrs. Obama was trying to get her children to eat more fruits and vegetables. It wasn't always easy,

but she stuck to it because she began to see results. But what if those juicy red tomatoes were growing right outside her door? What if Malia and Sasha could pick them just minutes before dinner? And what if they had helped plant those tomatoes, and the cucumbers, too?

They'd understand more about their food, they'd be more interested in their salads, they'd eat more good things, their mother thought. But first there was no time in her busy Chicago life; and then, after she had put aside her job, she was on the road campaigning with her husband. Again, there wasn't any time for the work a garden requires.

"So I thought, what a nice idea if we got to the White House and could plant a garden right in our backyard there," she recalled when her kitchen garden in Washington, D.C. started to take shape.

After Barack Obama won the presidential election of 2008, his wife began to expand her vision of an ideal garden. She took note of activists such as Roger Doiron, whose petition to plant a kitchen garden at the White House gathered over 100,000 signatures. Mrs. Obama wanted her garden to do more than feed her family and even the White House staff.

She hoped to help educate a nation with it. She wanted to help other families learn what her own daughters eventually found out: As Mrs. Obama put it, "A carrot that comes right out of the ground is actually kind of sweet and tasty, and it tastes a little different from carrots you get in a store."

If she started by focusing family attention on the glory of a fresh carrot, the results could lead to a nation of healthier, slimmer children and adults with lower rates of diabetes and clogged arteries.

The stunning idea of a White House kitchen garden took much planning.

Planting a garden with an eye to the public was not unprecedented. After John Quincy Adams took office in 1825 and planted two acres of vegetables, herbs and fruit trees, he wrote, "Now I shall plant, if at all, more for the public than myself."

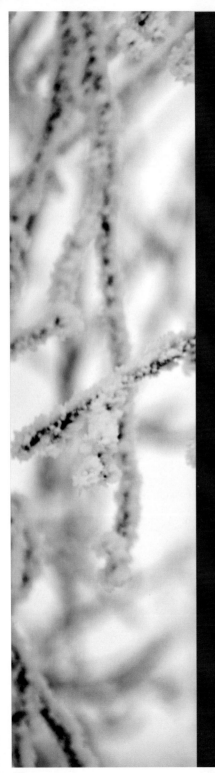

One question was where to place the new kitchen garden.

Abraham Lincoln grew strawberries, lettuce, carrots and celery in his White House garden which more or less occupied the space that John Quincy Adams had claimed. Would that Lincoln had grown enough to feed an army — Civil War troops occasionally camped on the South Lawn, and begged for food from the White House kitchen.

The kitchen garden of Lincoln's time was torn up in 1871 to make way for the construction of what is now the West Wing.

Michelle Obama chose a sunny spot on the South Lawn, tucked behind the tennis court and the South Fountain, and within sight of the iron fence along E Street that pedestrians peek through. She wanted her kitchen garden to have a public aspect but not dominate the classic view.

She also wished to be a caretaker of what already existed outside her taxpayer-supported home, and consulted Jim Adams, chief horticulturalist of the White House, and she talked with its groundskeepers. None of the historic trees and plantings on the White House ground had to be removed to create the 1,100-square-foot, L-shaped kitchen-garden plot.

Another big question: What to plant? Sam Kass, a White House chef, and now also Food Initiative Coordinator, helped her decide. She chose what Americans most like to plant: Tomatoes are the most popular home-grown vegetable, followed by cucumbers, sweet peppers, beans and carrots, according to the National Gardening Association. Mrs. Obama planted those and she put in other vegetables to her family's taste. She also included edibles that represented diverse tastes in this big country that would do well in the D.C. climate. A wide variety of herbs was essential to her cooks and herself. She also included berries.·

By the time the workers came out in overalls, boots and gloves to measure the borders for the garden plots, a lot of the hard work — dreaming up a garden that could be a model to the nation — had been done.

MANY GARDENS START WITH A DREAM. WHAT'S YOURS?

Some envision warm soil sifting thru their fingers; some see vibrant tomatoes.

PART II

A Time to Sow

In mid-March, the capital's famous cherry blossoms were in full flower. And Michelle Obama, honorary chair of the National Cherry Blossom Festival, found the time ripe to prepare her garden. On March 20, 26 fifth-graders from the nearby Bancroft Elementary School joined her to help get the soil ready for planting. The school has its own garden, so the students were somewhat familiar with the work required.

"This is a big day for us," said Michelle Obama, welcoming the kids to the garden. "So I want to thank you, guys." Mrs. Obama, wearing black pants and a black sweater, picked up a shovel and got to work along with chef Sam Kass, also passionate about kitchen gardens. They and the student volunteers scraped up the grass and put it in wheelbarrows, then they spread mulch on the ground. Mulch helps retain moisture and control weeds. On this sunny and breezy first day of spring, there was still enough snap in the air for the children to wear coats, though they went without hats. The commemorative trees on the White House grounds — one planted by each president since Rutherford B. Hayes was president in 1878 — were beginning to bud. Later, the kids sat at picnic tables and ate shovel-shaped cookies baked in the White House kitchen.

Another day, Kass and the garden crew did more to prepare the garden, running a noisy roto-tiller over the garden beds to turn over six to eight inches of soil at a time. Then they added nutrients, including crab meal made from crabs that lived in the nearby Cheseapeake Bay. These make the soil more balanced and fertile, better for growing vegetables.

THE JEFFERSON PLOT

Michelle Obama instructed the White House garden team to save room for a special plot of vegetables sent from the garden that Thomas Jefferson had started at Monticello, his Virginia home. Jefferson, an avid gardener, cultivated 250 varieties of vegetables at Monticello and was the first to hire a gardener to till a garden at the White House.

"Thomas Jefferson, more than any one man, changed the way we eat in this country and the way we grow food," said Sam Kass in a video about the White House Kitchen Garden. "He's the first person to start seasonal growing. That is something that people are coming back to now, thinking about ways to use a diversity of crops and keep growing throughout the year."

The Thomas Jefferson Bed, tucked between a plot of spinach and peas, and another of fennel, was planted with some of Jefferson's favorite vegetables, rare by today's standards: prickly-seeded spinach (with spiny seeds but plain leaves); tennis ball lettuce (a delicate predecessor to today's Boston lettuce); Savoy cabbage. Nearby is a descendant of a Marseilles fig plant that Jefferson described as "incomparably superior to any fig I have seen."

In the Jefferson plot is a marker that contains Jefferson's thoughts on gardening:

by Charles Willson Peale, 1791

"I have often thought that if heaven had given me choice of my position and calling, it should have been on a rich spot of earth, well watered, and near a good market for the productions of the garden. No occupation is so delightful to me as the culture of the earth, the failure of one thing repaired by the success of another, and instead of one harvest a continued one through the year."

FIRST PICKINGS

When the Bancroft children made their second garden visit, they were ready to plant herbs, lettuce, kale and chard. Before they got to work, the First Lady asked the group why they thought they were planting fruits and vegetables. One fifth-grader said, "So you can be healthy." Another said fruits and vegetables give you energy, and a third said they can make you strong.

"It can make you strong — yes, absolutely," responded Mrs. Obama. "This is one of the main reasons we're doing this. What I've learned as a mom, in trying to feed my girls, is that it is so important for them to get regular fruits and vegetables in their diets, because [they] have nutrients, [they] do make you strong, [they are] brain food."

At this session, the First Lady did not worry about getting down and dirty. She used a trowel as she worked with two girls to plant dill, rosemary, thyme and cilantro. The girls dug the holes, and then Mrs. Obama, on her hands and knees, gently dropped in the plants and helped pat the dirt around the roots. After the girls returned with watering cans, Mrs. Obama admitted that the work was "easier than ripping the grass up."

After the children left, the garden needed to do its own work of growing in the sunlight and warm spring weather of Washington, D.C. It wouldn't be long before the first herbs and leafy greens would be big enough to harvest.

White House Baked Eggs with Swiss Chard
Serves 8

CHARD

Chard is filled with Vitamin A. Just one cup of cooked chard contains twice the amount that you are supposed to eat in a day.

The White House spring plantings included both red and green chard. The variety with reddish leaves and stalks has a stronger flavor than the green variety.

Eating this is a bit like eating green eggs — without the ham. This dish is a good way to start the day, unless your children, taking a cue from the obstinate Dr. Seuss character, Sam, will not eat it here or there or anywhere.

6 large eggs
Salt and pepper, to taste
13/4 cups potatoes diced into small pieces
2 cups Swiss chard (or other leafy greens)
1/2 tablespoon butter
11/2 teaspoons vegetable oil
1 cup grated cheddar cheese
1 cup cooked turkey breakfast sausage (sliced, diced or chopped)

1. Preheat the oven to 300 degrees.
2. In a bowl, beat the eggs. Season them to taste with salt and pepper.
3. Wash the chard and tear it into smaller pieces.
4. Warm an oven-proof sauté pan over medium heat. (The pan should not get too hot.) Add the oil and butter. Add the potatoes and chard, and sauté until the potatoes begin to soften, about 6-10 minutes. Remove the vegetables from the pan and set aside.
5. In the same sauté pan, pour in the eggs to form a base, and continue heating over medium. When the eggs begin to cook, place the cooked potatoes, Swiss chard and sausage on top, using a spoon to distribute them evenly. Add the cheese.
6. Place the pan in the oven to finish cooking the eggs and melt the cheese, about 15 minutes. Remove from the oven and cut into wedges to serve.

CHICKPEAS

Chehalis, Washington, located about halfway between Seattle and Portland, Oregon, is a temperate place where Swiss chard grows super fast and abundantly almost all year long. This soup recipe is easy to make because you only have to chop one vegetable — the onion. Many families in the area near Blue Earth Farms have adopted it. Popular brands of hot chili sauce are El Pato, Sriracha and Frank's Red Hot.

1 large onion
4 cloves garlic
1 (15 ounce) can chickpeas (or substitute black beans or other types of beans)
2 tablespoons olive oil
1 tablespoon butter
1 bunch (approximately 1 pound) Swiss chard or spinach, washed and torn into bite-sized pieces
4 cups (24 ounces) chopped canned tomatoes
1-2 teaspoons chili sauce
2 cups vegetable or chicken broth
1 cup crumbled feta cheese or sour cream

1. Peel and chop the onion. Press the garlic in a garlic press. Put a colander in the sink and empty the canned chickpeas to drain, and rinse them under cold water. Leave them in the colander while you make the rest of the recipe.

2. In a large soup pot over medium-high heat, heat the olive oil and butter until they melt together. Add the onion and garlic. Saute until the onion turns from white to translucently clear (about 10 minutes). Stir frequently and lower the heat on the stove if the vegetables start burning.

3. Add the chard or spinach to the pot. The leaves should come almost to the top of the pot, but they will shrink when they cook. Cook, stirring until the greens begin to wilt, about 2-3 minutes.

4. Add the tomatoes, chili sauce, and chickpeas. Cook, stirring, for 2-3 minutes more.

5. Add the broth (it should cover all the vegetables), and let the soup heat up until it boils. Then lower the heat on the stove to a simmer (barely boiling) and cook for 15 minutes. Turn off the stove and move the pot to a safe spot away from the burner.

6. When you serve the soup, put the feta cheese or sour cream in a small bowl. Let each person put a little bit on top of the soup.

– Blue Earth Farms, Chehalis, WA

KALE

Kale is one of the hardier vegetables that you can grow. It doesn't seem to mind the cold of a chilly spring or fall day, and even tastes sweeter after a frost. The frilly leaves feel sturdy, too. Black kale, the variety grown at the White House, is also called Tuscan kale because it originated in Italy. Its dark, crinkly leaves have a slightly peppery flavor.

One type of kale can generally substitute for another in recipes, although flowering kale, which grows in white and purple heads, is considered too tough to eat at all.

This recipe makes it easy to use kale because it requires no cooking. Noah Sheetz, executive chef at the New York Executive Mansion in Albany, says he makes it quite often with gardening groups that include parents and kids, as he spreads the word that cooking with locally-grown food is fun. In fact, he got the recipe from Youth Organics, a youth and agriculture program near the governor's mansion.

This dish is also popular with From the Ground Up, a gardening program at the Marbletown Elementary School in New York's Hudson Valley.

The downside of the recipe is that you have to scrub your hands twice: Before you start it, and after you finish — because your hands are then oily.

You can easily add other ingredients to this salad. Try chopped fresh garlic or herbs, red bell pepper slices, shredded carrots or radishes.

Nicci Cagan, one of the founders of From the Ground Up, says her daughter likes to mix the salad with a mashed avocado. You could even add a spoonful of the kale salad to an omelet.

10 large kale leaves
Salt, for sprinkling
1 tablespoon olive oil
Juice from 1/2 lemon

1. Wash the kale leaves and place them on a clean dishtowel or on paper towels. Pat dry.
2. Set out a large bowl. Use your hands to tear the tough stems from the center of the kale leaves. Discard the stems. Tear the remaining parts of the kale leaves into bite-sized pieces. You should have about 3 packed cups of kale leaves. Place them in the bowl.
3. Sprinkle the leaves with salt. Add the olive oil.
4. Using your hands, mix the olive oil and salt into the leaves, rubbing the leaves between your fingers so the oil really works into the leaves. Keep mixing until all the leaves are coated with oil and salt.
5. Add the lemon juice (you can squeeze the lemon right over the bowl, but use a sieve so the seeds don't get in). Toss the leaves with the lemon juice. Serve as a side dish.

— Noah Sheetz
Albany, NY

2 pounds collards (or substitute chard, mustard greens or kale)
2 cloves garlic
2 tablespoons butter
Salt and pepper, to taste

Even elementary-school kids eat their vegetables when they help make these sautéed greens, proclaims Seth Freedman, manager of the Atlanta garden program who contributed this recipe. He said, "They get so much joy out of harvesting the greens that they have cared for in the garden. And preparing them involves one of the all-time favorite kitchen tools: the salad spinner!"

He adds, "After all that hard work, almost every single student eats the greens like candy, with lots of 'mmmm-mms' and 'yummys'!"

GARLIC

1. Wash the collard or other greens in water, handling gently so you don't bruise them. Remove the stems from the greens and tear into pieces about 2 inches square.
2. Cut the garlic cloves into thin slices.
3. Place a large pan over medium-low heat. Add the butter and let it melt.
4. Add the garlic. Cook until it starts to get soft, about 1-2 minutes, but do not let it brown. Its aroma will fill your kitchen!
5. Add the greens. Stir as the greens wilt. Add the salt and pepper.
6. Cook until tender (the cooking time will depend on which greens you are using), adding more water if the pan begins to get dry. Taste, add more salt and pepper if you like, and serve.

—— Seeds of Nutrition
Atlanta, GA,
part of the Mendoza Foundation

California Girl E'mya Atkins, age 8, picks collards in an East Bay garden.

Oakland Based Urban Gardens (O.B.U.G.S.)

SCALLIONS

This is an easy recipe to toss together from whatever comes up in the spring. You can substitute a handful of fresh spinach for the kale. The stir-fry became an Urban Sprouts signature dish because it comes together so quickly that nobody has to wait too long to eat! Look for rice vinegar and sesame oil at an Asian market or in the Asian section of a supermarket.

Sauce:
1/3 **cup soy sauce or tamari**
2 **tablespoons rice vinegar**
1 **teaspoon sesame oil**
1 **teaspoon sugar**
1 **teaspoon rice wine (optional)**

Vegetables:
2-3 **onions**
2 **cloves garlic**
4 **scallions, including green stems**
8 **leaves kale or other leafy greens**
1/2 **pound broccoli**
1/2 **pound snow peas**
1 **tablespoon vegetable or peanut oil**
1 **tablespoon peeled and minced fresh ginger**
1 **tablespoon water**

Tip: To make more of an entrée, stir fry chicken pieces, shrimp or small tofu chunks separately and add them at the end.

For the sauce:
In a small bowl, mix together all sauce ingredients. Set aside.

For the vegetables:
1. Prepare the vegetables and line them up near the stove so you can quickly stir-fry. Dice the onion. You should have enough for 2 cups. Mince the garlic or run it through a garlic press. Wash and chop the scallions. Wash the kale, remove the tough stems, and tear it into bite-sized pieces. Separate the broccoli tops into small florets. Wash the snow peas and remove the tough stem ends and the stringy piece that runs up the center.
2. Place a wok or deep frying pan on the stove over high heat. After 1-2 minutes, carefully add the oil and swirl it around. Add the onions and stir-fry for 2 minutes. Add the garlic, scallions and ginger, and stir-fry for 30 seconds.
3. Add the greens, broccoli and snow peas, plus the sauce. Stir-fry for 1 minute. Add the water, cover the wok, and steam for 1 minute. Serve with rice.

—Urban Sprouts
San Francisco, CA

Under a warm Bay Area sky, three Urban Sprout kids heat kale and collard greens for the stir fry they're preparing in the Garden for the Environment.

Abby Jaramillo

If your spring vegetables are just coming into season and you don't have a large crop of any one thing, this recipe from The Edible Schoolyard fits the bill. This program, part of the Chez Panisse Foundation founded by chef and food activist Alice Waters, was one of the pioneers in connecting gardening to education.

Since it started at the Martin Luther King Middle School in Berkeley, California in 1995, the Edible Schoolyard (ESY) has expanded to New Orleans and created a network of affiliates around the country. Students here literally have a hand in bringing their food from field to table.

4 cloves garlic
3 tablespoons olive oil
1 tablespoon peeled and minced fresh ginger
5 cups assorted washed and chopped vegetables (such as chard, bok choy, tat soy, carrots, scallions, celery, peas and squash)
5 cups cold cooked rice
2 teaspoons smoked sesame oil (available at Asian supermarkets)
5 eggs
1/4 cup soy sauce
Salt and pepper, to taste

1. Peel and mince the garlic.
2. In a large skillet with a heavy bottom, heat the olive oil over medium heat. Add the garlic and ginger; cook for 30 seconds.
3. Add the assorted vegetables and cook for about 5 minutes. They should still be a little crisp.
4. Add the rice and sesame oil. Stir to combine.
5. In a bowl, lightly beat the eggs with a fork or a whisk. When the rice is hot, add the eggs and soy sauce, cooking until the eggs are dry.
6. Season with salt and pepper.

— The Edible Schoolyard
Berkeley, CA

Clara Silverstein

FRESHFARM Market near the White House: kale in foreground, chard behind

LETTUCES

Four types were planted in the garden in the early spring: Green Oak Leaf, Red Romaine, Butterhead and Speckled for a variety of leaf shapes, colors and flavors. A salad served at a meeting of President Obama with his top economic advisors was one of the first dishes to be made from lettuce harvested in the garden.

Almost any kind of lettuce makes a good start for a salad. The next step is to add vegetables and herbs that are in season. Look for an assortment of colors and flavors. Elementary school kids in the Camden City Garden Program in New Jersey's GrowLab throw a salad party each year and make a "Rainbow in My Plate." They pick tomatoes for red, carrots for orange, yellow peppers or corn for yellow, lettuce, broccoli or cucumbers for green, blueberries for blue, and grapes or eggplant for purple.

Some of the contestants on "The Biggest Loser," NBC's weight-loss reality show, need encouragement to eat salads instead of junk food. White House chef Sam Kass was up to the task when he helped a visiting "Loser" hopeful make a salad that almost no one can get enough of.

This is a family-size adaptation of the winning salad mix and dressing.

Salad:
1 head of fresh lettuce
1 cucumber
**2 fresh in-season
  tomatoes**
1/4 red onion
1 bunch fresh basil

Dressing:
1/3 cup olive oil
**4 tablespoons
  lemon juice**
1 teaspoon honey
Salt and pepper, to taste

For the salad:
1. Wash and dry the lettuce. Tear it into bite-size pieces. Peel the cucumber and cut it into bite-sized bits. Wash the tomatoes and cut them into bite-sized pieces. Peel the onion and slice it as thin as possible. Wash and chop the basil into large pieces.
2. In a large mixing bowl, combine the lettuce, cucumbers, tomatoes, onions and basil. Toss together so the ingredients are well mixed.

For the dressing:
Place the dressing ingredients in a container with a tight-fitting lid. Cover the container and shake vigorously. Add the dressing to the salad, toss and serve immediately.

Springtime is salad time in Pittsburgh, at a program modelled on Alice Waters' famous garden in Berkeley, California. The Pennsylvania children cut up the lettuce they grew then added sugar snap peas, carrots, broccoli and chives to the salad bowl, before tossing everything in a vinaigrette dressing they'd also made. It's likely that more than one kid loved their achievement enough to introduce it to mom or dad.

A discerning eater wouldn't even think of sprinkling black pepper from a shaker into the dressing. It will taste much livelier when you use freshly-ground peppercorns.

Dressing:
1/2 cup olive oil
1/4 cup red wine vinegar
Sea salt, to taste
Freshly ground black pepper, to taste

Salad:
4-6 cups freshly-harvested lettuce leaves
1/2 cup sugar snap peas
1 carrot
1/2 cup broccoli florets
1 tablespoon snipped fresh chives

For the dressing: Place the dressing ingredients in a small bowl and mix with a whisk or a fork. Set aside.

For the salad:
1. Wash the lettuce, gently tear it into bite-sized pieces, and place them in a bowl. Wash the peas and break them in half. Peel the carrot and cut it into bite-sized pieces. Wash the broccoli. Put the peas, carrot and broccoli into the bowl. Sprinkle the chives over the top.
2. Whisk the dressing again, then pour it over the salad (you may not need it all), toss everything together, and serve.

— Grow Pittsburgh,
Edible Schoolyard Program
Pittsburgh, PA

LEAFY WRAPS

DANIEL AND ANNIE'S SALAD WRAPS
Serves 6

Wrap a green leaf around a vegetable filling, and you have a salad that can be eaten with one hand.

Many gardening groups make some version of this easy, no-cook snack. At the Camden Children's Garden in New Jersey, Roughage Roll-Ups (roughage is fiber---the part of food that your body doesn't digest but is still good for your gastro tract) became a popular snack for teens in a job training program, said consultant Tracy Tomchik. Everyone started by gathering whatever veggies were in season, such as broccoli, chives, dill, peas, shallots or turnips. Once these were washed and chopped, the kids sprinkled them with grated cheese, herbs or salad dressing for flavor, then rolled them up in the biggest, sturdiest leaves they could find from spinach, Romaine lettuce or cooked cabbage.

The students at Maha Farm in Clinton Valley, Washington, rolled up baby carrots or peas (or both) in large French sorrel leaves. They ate them straight up, farm owner Anza Muenchow reports, or dipped them into whatever was handy, such as salad dressing, cheese spread or hummus.

There's more to the Bronx than city streets and subways roaring under them. This borough of New York is home to a spectacular botanical garden, so large that a wide river runs through it. There is also plenty of room for vegetable gardens. Families and kids who plant in this Bronx garden also get to eat there—even some of the flowers.

6 lettuce leaves,
  plus 6 more for
  slicing
1 kohlrabi bulb
  or 1 cup
  shredded cabbage
5 radishes
6 scallions
6 mint or basil
  leaves (or more
  to taste)
Edible flowers, to
  garnish (such as
  Johnny jump-ups,
  chives or nastur
  tiums), optional

1. Wash and dry the lettuce leaves. Peel and slice the kohlrabi. Wash and dice the radishes. Wash the scallions, and cut off and discard the root ends.
2. Lay out 6 lettuce leaves on a countertop or a large plate. With scissors, cut the remaining 6 leaves into ribbons. Into each lettuce leaf, lay some kohlrabi and radishes, 1 scallion (cut it in half if it's too long), and 1 mint or basil leaf. Roll it up. If necessary, pin closed with a toothpick. Garnish the top with edible flowers. Serve with your favorite dressing as a dip.

— Ruth Rea Howell Family Garden
New York Botanical Garden
Bronx, NY

Chives in Flower

1 lettuce leaf
1 tablespoon each of any of the following: chopped apples, chopped celery, walnuts or pecans, raisins or dried cranberries
1 tablespoon vanilla yogurt

Robin Schell, school garden coordinator of Rural Resources in Greeneville, Tennessee (also home of the Andrew Johnson National Historic site), had a tough sales job when she suggested this recipe. The children weren't sure they wanted to try something new, but since they grew the lettuce, they all agreed to take a bite. "In the end, nothing was left! They ate it all and have been asking when they can make it again," she said. The combination of ingredients is sort of a Waldorf salad to go. Add and subtract to these ingredients according to what you like.

1. Pick the largest, most pliable lettuce leaves that you can find. Leaf lettuces work really well for this.
2. Rinse the lettuce leaves in cold water and pat dry between sheets of paper towels.
3. Add spoonfuls of chopped apples, chopped celery, walnuts or pecans, and raisins or dried cranberries in the center of the leaf. Each person can choose their own mix of ingredients.
4. Add a dollop of vanilla yogurt.
5. Fold the lettuce lengthwise over the toppings and then fold up the ends, like a burrito or little package. Pick up and eat!

— Tusculum View Elementary School
after school program
Rural Resources
Greeneville, TN

Johnny jump-up

28

TEAM TUSCULUM

Their lettuce and herbs are a match for any lettuce-wrap treats.

Rural Resources

SALAD DRESSINGS

BALSAMIC VINAIGRETTE SALAD DRESSING
Makes about ¾ cup

One of the most enthusiastic participants in a Richmond, Virginia, program, six-year-old Coran, spent most of his time munching on whatever greens he was allowed to pick from the garden. "I love raw mustard greens because they make my tongue burn!" he let everyone know.

Not everyone, age six or 60, agreed with him on this point, but almost all the kids had a good time devising salad dressings from oil, vinegar, fresh crushed garlic and "whatever herbs we decided to throw in," said horticulturalist Allison Mesnard, who worked with the younger gardeners in the kitchen as well as in the vegetable patch.

2 cloves garlic
1/2 cup olive oil
1/4 cup balsamic (or apple cider) vinegar
Approximately 1 teaspoon chopped fresh oregano or 1/2 teaspoon dried
1/2 to 1 tablespoon Dijon mustard (optional)
A sprinkling of chopped fresh herbs, such as basil, dill or marjoram (optional)

1. Peel the garlic cloves. Place on a cutting board and crush with the back of a wooden spoon.
2. Place the garlic and the remaining ingredients in a quart-sized canning jar or another container with a tight-fitting lid. Cover and shake vigorously. Pour or spoon onto your salad.

Tip: The flavor improves when dressing is allowed to sit for awhile. Store leftover dressing in the refrigerator.

—— Tricycle Gardens and
Neighborhood Resource Center
Children's Learning Garden
Richmond, VA

DILL

This plant grows so fast that it's often called a dill weed. Its seeds flavor sour pickles.

Through the Georgia Organics Chef to School program with Cathy Conway of Avalon Catering, the children made a buttermilk ranch dressing dip to go with the fresh vegetables that they grew in their garden. They dipped carrots, tomatoes, cucumbers, and radishes into it, but the dip complements almost any kind of crunchy raw vegetable. Keep everyone from reaching into the same bowl by giving each person a little bit of dressing for their plate, or use the dip as a salad dressing.

In a small bowl, place all the ingredients and whisk until blended. Enjoy with freshly picked vegetables or on a salad.

— Mary Lin Elementary School
Atlanta, GA

Tip: Turn this into blue cheese dressing by adding about ¼ cup of crumbled Roquefort cheese.

3/4 **cup mayonnaise**
1/2 **cup buttermilk**
2 **tablespoons finely chopped fresh parsley**
2 **tablespoons finely chopped celery leaves**
11/2 **teaspoons fresh lemon juice**
11/2 **teaspoons Dijon mustard**
3/4 **teaspoon onion powder**
1/4 **teaspoon dried dill**

31

RHUBARB

Perennial rhubarb is ready before anything green in many parts of the States. It's a truly sour fruit; many people call rhubarb the "pie plant" because it is so often used in a lattice-topped pie. It looks like pink celery, but is so tart that most people need to dip it or stew it in sugar before they can eat it in or out of a pie. In much of the northeast, partaking of a rhubarb pie for dessert is a Yankee rite of spring.

One way to cut down on (but not eliminate) the sugar required to draw out rhubarb's deliciousness is to simmer chunks of it with sweet strawberries. Rhubarb lasts a while and is often around when the first strawberries appear. After the White House donated some of its rhubarb harvest to nearby Miriam's Kitchen, which gives food to the poor, a volunteer pastry chef at Miriam's made it into a sauce with strawberries, served for breakfast as a topping for French toast.

RHUBARB PIE
Makes 1 9-inch pie

Mrs. Obama also praised rhubarb when she visited the Bancroft School in May. It's hard to go wrong with rhubarb as long as you remember to chop off and dispose of its leaves, which can make you ill, and you have sweetener on hand.

After the muted colors of a garden in winter, the red of rhubarb and strawberry are especially welcome. Both flavors inform every bite of this pie from Gaining Ground farm in Concord, Massachusetts. To make the pie without strawberries, increase the rhubarb by one cup and add a little more sugar. For a treat, serve each slice with ice cream or whipped cream. For something healthier, top with plain or vanilla yogurt.

Crust (makes 2 9-inch crusts):
1 cup (2 sticks) unsalted butter
1/2 cup water
2 cups all-purpose flour
1 teaspoon salt, preferably Kosher (see note on next page)

Filling:
3 cups 1/2-inch pieces of rhubarb
1 cup hulled and sliced strawberries
1 cup sugar, or to taste
1/4 cup small pearl tapioca, such as Minute brand
1 egg
1 tablespoon flour
1 tablespoon butter

For the crust:

1. Using a sharp knife on a cutting board, cut the butter into small squares. Place it in a bowl and return it to the refrigerator for about 30 minutes to allow it to firm up again.
2. Fill a measuring cup with ½ cup of water. Add ice cubes to keep the water very cold.
3. In a large bowl, whisk together the flour and salt. Add the chilled butter. Toss it with a fork so that each piece of butter becomes coated. With a pastry cutter or your clean hands, work the butter into the flour until the mixture resembles coarse meal.
4. Add the ice water one tablespoon at a time and stir the mixture with a fork until the dough comes together. You may not need the entire ½ cup of ice water.
5. Remove the dough from the bowl and separate it into two equal-sized pieces. Form each piece into a disk. With the heel of your hand, gently press on the dough to ensure that all ingredients are incorporated.
6. Wrap each disk of dough in plastic wrap and refrigerate for at least 30 minutes until ready to roll out for your pie.

For the filling:

1. Preheat the oven to 450 degrees.
2. In a bowl, place the rhubarb, strawberries, sugar, and tapioca. Stir and let sit for at least 15 minutes, stirring occasionally.
3. In the meantime, on a clean work surface, roll out one of the dough disks to about 10 inches in diameter. Gently fit it into a 9-inch pie pan. Cut off any dough that hangs over the sides of the pan. Roll out the other disk and cut it into strips about ½ inch wide for making a lattice crust (a lattice allows moisture to escape so the pie won't be runny).
4. In a small bowl, beat the egg. Stir it into the rhubarb mixture, then pour the rhubarb mixture into the pie plate. Cut the butter into small pieces. Sprinkle the top of the filling with the flour, then dot with the butter.
5. Place half the strips of crust across the top of the pie, then weave the other half through. Or put half the strips across the pie vertically, and half across horizontally. Attach the end of each strip by pressing it against the bottom crust and pinching it together.
6. Bake the pie for 15 minutes. Lower the temperature to 300 degrees. Continue baking for at least 45 minutes, until the crust is brown and the fruit is bubbling hot. As it cools, the juices will firm up.

Note: Kosher salt is a coarser grind of salt than regular salt, with a cleaner flavor because it is not iodized. If you can't find it, use regular salt.

–– from the *Gaining Ground Table*
Gaining Ground
Concord, MA

RHUBARB–STRAWBERRY COMPOTE
Serves 4-6

Carolyn Blount Brodersen gardens with her husband and six-year-old daughter, Jaclyn Sachiyo Brodersen. Carolyn cooks with kids at her daughter's school and with her family at home.

Her family, and the kids she works with, have found that rhubarb and strawberries go together like peanut butter and jelly. Jaclyn described her favorite recipe as "rhubarb chopped up with melted strawberries," adding, "We eat it straight, without ice cream. It's not good — it's great!"

But if you like, you can serve it over ice cream, pancakes, waffles or cheese blintzes. You can even stir it into yogurt or use it as a layer in parfaits.

3 cups strawberries (about 1 pound)
4 to 6 stalks rhubarb (about 1 pound)
3/4 cup sugar
2 teaspoons cornstarch
1/4 cup orange juice
1 teaspoon vanilla

1. Cut the stems off the strawberries, and then cut each in half lengthwise. Remove all the leaves from the rhubarb stalks and trim off the root ends. Slice the remaining stalks into ½ inch pieces.
2. In a pot, mix the sugar and the cornstarch. Add the strawberries, rhubarb, orange juice and vanilla. Cover the pot and cook on the stove over medium heat, stirring gently and only occasionally, until rhubarb is soft, about 15 minutes. Be careful not to stir too much or too vigorously, as you don't want to break up the rhubarb into too many strings and you want to preserve the shape of the strawberries.
3. Remove from the stove and let the compote cool before serving.

Carolyn Blount Brodersen
Ventura, CA

Carolyn Brodersen and her daughter Jaclyn are berry-happy co-chefs.

It might seem strange to mix tart rhubarb with equally tart buttermilk, but this cake comes out moist and sweet, with a sugary crust on top. It also gives your kitchen a wonderful cinnamon aroma as it cooks. "It is fabulous!" said Susan Medlin, director of an Idaho culinary program. The recipe comes from a student's grandmother. In the Urban Garden School kitchen, it is made with organic ingredients, and the oven is turned on after some of the ingredients are mixed to save energy. Kids in the program help serve 600-700 lunches during spring and summer.

Tip: If you don't have buterilk for the following recipe, you can fix-up regular milk: Add 1 tablespoon of lemon juice or white vinegar (no other color). Stir and wait 5 minutes until milk bubbles on top. Stir again. The doctored-milk is a good sub for buttermilk.

RHUBARB BUTTERMILK CAKE
Serves 12

Approximately 1/2 pound rhubarb (enough for 2 cups chopped rhubarb)
2 cups unbleached flour
1 teaspoon baking soda
1/2 cup (1 stick) unsalted butter, left out on the counter to soften
1 1/2 cups brown sugar
1 egg
1 cup buttermilk
1/2 cup white sugar
1 teaspoon cinnamon

1. Grease a 9-by-13-inch baking pan (oven-safe glass works best for this recipe) by rubbing it with a little butter or spraying it with non-stick cooking spray.
2. Wash the rhubarb stalks and chop off the leaves. Starting from one end, chop across each stalk into pieces about ½ inch long. You may need to cut an extra-fat rhubarb stalk in half the long way. Measure out two cups of cut rhubarb and put the rhubarb in a bowl. Set aside.
3. In a small bowl, sift together the flour and baking soda. Set aside.
4. Place the butter and brown sugar in a large bowl. Using an electric mixer, cream the butter and sugar together until the mixture is no longer chunky, but quite smooth. Add the egg and keep mixing until well blended.

5. Preheat the oven to 350 degrees.
6. Put the buttermilk in a measuring cup with a spout or in a pitcher.
7. Add about ½ cup of the flour mixture to the bowl with the butter-egg mixture. Using the mixer on medium speed, mix in the flour. Add about ¼ cup of the buttermilk, mixing to combine everything. Stop the mixer and scrape the side of the bowl with a spoon once or twice as you mix so you make sure to get everything into the batter. Continue adding ½ cup of flour, and then ¼ cup of the buttermilk, until all the ingredients are mixed. Don't keep beating or you will have a tough cake.
8. Add the chopped rhubarb to the batter and mix it in with a spoon.
9. Pour the batter into the baking pan, smoothing the top evenly with the back of the spoon.
10. In a small bowl, mix the white sugar with the cinnamon, and sprinkle on top of the batter. It will cover the batter.
11. Put the pan in the oven and bake for 30 minutes, until brown. Check by carefully pulling the cake from the oven (use mitts) and inserting a toothpick into the center of the cake, then pulling it out. The toothpick should not have batter on it if the cake is done.
12. Remove the cake from the oven. Serve while the cake is just slightly warm but not hot. For a special treat put whipped cream or vanilla ice cream on top. Plain or vanilla-flavored yogurt makes a good topping, too.

— Boise Urban Garden School (BUGS)
Boise, ID

THE HERBS OF SPRING

THYME

In the springtime White House Garden, dill, thyme, rosemary and cilantro were all coming along, thanks to the rain followed by warm weather. Thyme clipped from early sprigs garnished a fish dish that was served in the White House's West Wing cafeteria. After that successful picking and serving, Kass and other White House chefs regularly went down to the garden to pick herbs to accent flavors and decorate plates. Herbs are a favorite at private First Family meals.

LEMON-THYME OR ROSEMARY-ORANGE SHORT-BREAD COOKIES   Makes about 28 cookies

Most of us don't think of a cookie as garden fresh, but these buttery morsels might change your mind. The basic butter and sugar can be flavored with any number of herbs. Try using rosemary and orange zest in place of the thyme and lemon. You could also stir 1/2 teaspoon of cinnamon, or approximately 1 tablespoon of chopped crystallized ginger, into any dough. Almost any combination goes. Make dough ahead for your own version of slice-and-bake cookies.

3/4 **cup (1 1/2 sticks) butter, left out on the counter for an hour or so to soften**
1/3 **cup sugar**
2 **teaspoons fresh thyme leaves**
1/2 **teaspoon lemon zest (the yellow part of a lemon peel)**
1/8 **teaspoon salt**
1 1/3 **cups flour**

1. In a small bowl, using a fork or an electric mixer, cream the sugar and butter until they blend together.
2. In another bowl, stir together the thyme, lemon zest, salt and flour.
3. Add the flour mixture to the butter mixture. Stir together, then mix with clean hands until a soft dough forms.
4. Put the dough on a clean counter or table top. Divide it in half. Roll each half into a log about 1 inch in diameter and 8 inches long. Wrap each log in waxed paper or plastic wrap and place in the refrigerator for at least 1 hour. Or put the wrapped dough into a plastic freezer bag and freeze for later use.
5. When you are ready to bake, preheat the oven to 375 degrees. Cover a cookie sheet with parchment paper (this keeps the cookies from sticking to the cookie sheet).
6. Place the dough on a cutting board. Starting at one end of the log, slice the dough into circles about ¼-inch thick. Lay each circle flat on the cookie sheet, leaving about 1 inch in between each cookie.
7. Place the cookie sheet in the oven and bake until the cookies are brown around the edges, 8 to 10 minutes. Use a spatula to transfer the cookies to a wire rack to let them cool.

—— From the Ground Up
Stone Ridge, NY

CILANTRO

The leaves of the coriander plant are called cilantro and sometimes also Chinese or Mexican parsley, reflecting the international appeal of this bright green herb.

This pesto is a distant cousin of the basil-themed pesto that you probably recognize from Italian cooking. It puts herbs and seasonings together in a blender, but there the resemblance ends. Cilantro has a flavor all its own, enhanced by peanut butter and honey. Toss a spoonful of this spread with pasta, or spread it on grilled chicken. Later in the summer, slice up some fresh tomatoes and make a sandwich with the pesto.

CILANTRO PESTO
Makes about ½ cup

1 cup cilantro leaves
1/2 cup parsley leaves
1 clove garlic
2 tablespoons peanut butter
1 tablespoon honey
3 tablespoons olive oil
1-2 tablespoons water
Salt, to taste
Dash Tabasco sauce or cayenne pepper (optional)

1. Wash the cilantro and parsley leaves; set them on a clean dish-towel or on paper towels to dry.
2. Peel the garlic. Put it in a blender or food processor. Add the peanut butter, honey, cilantro and parsley. Turn on the motor and, with the motor running, drizzle in the olive oil until the mixture blends together. Drizzle in the water, a tablespoon at a time, if it still seems too thick and stubbornly sticks to the sides of the blender.
3. Put the pesto in a bowl. Stir in salt and Tabasco, if using.

1/2 **cup (1 stick) butter**
3 **cups flour**
4 **teaspoons baking powder**
4 **tablespoons sugar**
1/2 **teaspoon salt**
4 **eggs**
1 **cup milk**
About 1/2 **cup chopped fresh herbs of your choice, such as dill, parsley, basil or a combination**

1. Preheat the oven to 375 degrees. Line 24 muffin tins with paper liners.
2. Melt the butter in a small saucepan, then set it aside.
3. In a mixing bowl, sift together the flour, baking powder, sugar and salt.
4. In another bowl, whisk together the eggs, milk, melted butter and herbs.
5. Pour the egg mixture into the flour mixture and stir just until combined. Spoon the batter into the muffin tins.
6. Bake about 25 minutes, until golden brown. Serve with butter or your favorite jam.

— Natick Community Organic Farm
Natick, MA

This muffin batter is fairly plain, so it lets the flavor of the herbs stand out. Play around with different combinations of herbs to see which ones you like best. When cooking instructor Natasha Tauscher and some young students made these, she served the muffins with butter mixed with herbs. "Some kids loved them and some kids thought they were too herby," she said. Fortunately, you can adjust the amount of herbs to taste.

ARUGULA

Small-leaf arugula was first planted shortly after the lettuces were in the White House Kitchen Garden. It is often used in salads, but arugula is in the mustard family. In England, it is called rocket, perhaps because it grows so fast!

Arugula grew in the garden from spring through fall. The White House served it with an eggplant potato salad at its first state dinner. Much earlier in the season adventurous families who garden together were eating arugula in innovative salads or cooking it with pasta.

ARUGULA AND PAPAYA SALAD
Serves 4

Just three miles north of the Mexican border, a savvy school group took advantage of the high desert climate to start its garden in October as a learning tool for students and families. Some of the very vegetables placed in the White House garden in March — leafy greens, lettuces, chard, arugula, spinach and kale — were planted in autumn beds that were covered with plastic to protect them from freezing night temperatures, while the hot sun of daytime allowed them to thrive.

When the children of Columbus, New Mexico, finally got to lift the covers, they cheered because the full plants were ready to be harvested, according to adult volunteer Helena Myers.

The salad they made was a cross-cultural delight, because arugula has kind of a sharp flavor, but the naturally sweet slices of semitropical papaya balance it out. With the olive oil, lime juice and cheese, this salad needs no extra dressing.

1 bunch (approximately 1 pound) arugula
1 medium (approximately 10 to 12 ounces) papaya (see note below)
Half of a fresh lime
1/2 cup crumbled feta cheese
1 tablespoon olive oil

1. Wash and dry the arugula. Tear it into bite-sized pieces and place in a serving bowl.
2. Place the papaya on a cutting board. Cut it in half through the stem end so you end up with a long oval shape, not a circle. Use a spoon to scoop out the round, black, slippery seeds. Cut the papaya into long strips and peel off the skin from each one. Then cut the flesh into bite-sized pieces. Place on top of the arugula.
3. Squeeze the lime juice over the papaya, squeezing through a sieve or the clean fingers of one hand to catch any seeds. Sprinkle the cheese on top. Drizzle with olive oil. Serve.

Note: If you can't get papaya, substitute honeydew melon or sections of Clementine oranges.
— Columbus Elementary School
Columbus NM

Ann Cooper's mission is to help make school lunches healthier and tastier. While Director of Nutrition Services in Berkeley, California, Chef Ann, with the help of the community, saw to it that each of Berkeley's 12 schools had an on-site garden, a cooking program and a lunchroom salad bar.

The greens in this quick and easy pasta dish might include arugula, spinach, watercress or endive. For a heartier meal, add roasted or grilled squash, eggplant, or peppers. This dish is easy to bring to school, too, because it tastes great at room temperature.

2/3 **pound penne pasta**
Salt for pasta water
2 tablespoons extra virgin olive oil
1 cup diced onion (approximately 1 medium onion)
1 clove garlic
2 cups arugula or other greens
1/4 **cup water**
21/4 **teaspoons lemon juice**
1/4 **teaspoon ground black pepper**
1/3 **cup crumbled feta cheese**

1. Fill a large pot with water. Put it on the stove and bring it to a boil over high heat. Add the salt and pasta and let the water boil until the pasta is al dente (cooked through but not mushy). Use the package directions as a guide to how long to let the pasta cook. Put a colander in the sink. Carefully pour the water and the pasta into the colander. Let the pasta drain and set it aside.

2. While the pasta is cooking, peel and dice the onion. Peel and mince the garlic. Wash the arugula and chop it into bite-sized pieces.

3. Heat the oil in a large sauté pan over medium heat. Add the onions and sauté until they are lightly browned. Add the garlic and cook for 2 minutes. Add the arugula and water, and cook for 3 more minutes. When the arugula has wilted, add the cooked pasta and toss to heat it all the way through.

4. Add the lemon juice and pepper, and toss again. Top with feta cheese and serve.

— from *Lunch Lessons* by Ann Cooper (Renegade Lunch Lady) and founder of Food Family Farming Foundation's Lunch Box Project Boulder, CO

COLLARD GREENS

Collard greens, a staple of soul food, have a long history in the African-American community. Though collards, part of the cabbage family, do not grow in Africa, the African slaves already knew how to cook greens. Traditional African-American recipes still call for the early technique of slowly simmering the greens with bacon or salt pork, then serving them with the juices, called "pot likker." Unlike some other leafy greens, vitamin-rich collards are inevitably served cooked. They're almost as inevitably delicious; fortunately, the rainy D.C. spring of the first Obama kitchen garden assured a good crop of collards along with chard and kale.

At the Dr. Martin Luther King Jr. Elementary School, one of 10 Cambridge, Massachusetts Public Schools where CitySprouts runs a gardening program, kids wrote the name of each crop they were growing on a popsicle stick. Leaves from kale and the more exotic tatsoi stuck up from the raised beds. All the weeds the kids pulled went right into the compost bin, which garden coordinator Francey Hart Slater described as "where the action happens." Francey said that this hearty, one-dish recipe is a favorite among CitySprouts interns, who clean the pot out every time they make it. They even got a retired science teacher, who claims not to eat green things, to eat a whole bowl and even declare he liked it!

If you grew (or bought) kale, spinach or chard, that vegetable can be substituted for the collards. If you don't have dill, try another fresh herb such as parsley or oregano. For another variation, sprinkle each serving with a little bit of grated cheddar or crumbled feta. This is truly a vegetable dish that wants you to have it your way.

1 large onion
2 tablespoons olive oil
1 bunch (12 ounces) collard greens
1 cup uncooked white rice
1 3/4 cups hot water
2 tablespoons minced fresh dill
1/2 teaspoon salt
1/4 teaspoon pepper
Hot sauce, for serving

1. Peel and chop the onion.
2. Heat the olive oil in a large saucepan over medium heat.
3. Add the chopped onions. Cook, stirring, for 5 minutes, until the onions become soft and turn clear or translucent.
4. Wash the greens well and pat dry. Remove the stems and chop or tear the leaves into bite-sized pieces.
5. Add the greens to the pan. Stir and cover the pan. Cook 10 minutes. You may need to lower the heat to keep the onions from burning.
6. Stir the rice into the greens, continuing to stir until the rice is coated with oil and starting to look cloudy, about 3 minutes.
7. Add the water, dill, salt and pepper. Bring to a boil and then reduce the heat to low. Cover the pot and cook for 15 minutes.
8. Check the rice. If it's almost done (most of the water is gone), remove the pot from the heat and let it rest, with the cover still on, for 5 more minutes.
9. Serve with hot sauce.

–– CitySprouts
Cambridge, MA

This recipe for greens from *The White House Cookbook*, 1894 is designed for almost any type of greens, including ones that we seldom eat today — cowslips, burdock, chicory and dandelions. It recommends that washing the greens in a pan of salted water, or better yet, letting them soak, will "free them from insects and worms." It also cautions against overcooking, which "wastes the tender substances of the leaves." Here is a modern adaptation of the recipe.

Salt, as needed
6 cups thoroughly washed and torn greens with tough stems removed (such as collards, chard or kale)
2 tablespoons butter
Pepper, to taste
Vinegar, taste (optional)

1. Fill a large pot halfway with water. Sprinkle in some salt. Over high heat, bring to a boil.
2. Add the greens and return to a boil. Continue boiling until the greens are tender, 5 to 20 minutes, depending on the type of greens used.
3. Drain in a colander set in a sink.
4. When the greens are cool enough to handle, chop them into small pieces. Return the greens to the pot over medium heat. Add the butter, salt, pepper and vinegar. Continue cooking, stirring frequently, until heated through.

SPINACH

You've already been given a number of recipes for green-leaf vegetables such as chard, kale and collards for which you could substitute spinach. But there are times when only the S-vegetable will do. You're probably familiar with the typical fresh spinach salad, garnished with chopped egg and bacon bits, and perhaps fresh or sautéed red onion, and dressed in vinaigrette.

If you're of a certain age, you almost certainly know that the sailor Popeye owed his bulging muscles to spinach consumed straight from the can. Spinach really is super-healthy so don't hesitate to pass the strength legend on to your kids or grand-kids. But actually, fresh spinach is the better (and an easy) base material.

And if your assistant cooks remain reluctant, here is a recent story to help make your case: As Philadelphia Phillies slugger Ryan Howard toured the White House garden, he held up what appeared to be a spinach leaf and said, "This is as raw as it gets right here, out of the ground." He took a bite and said, "That's good!"

WHITE HOUSE NO-CREAM CREAMED SPINACH
Serves 6

One of Michelle Obama's favorite healthy spinach recipes is a creamy-style spinach made without cream by White House Executive Chef Cristeta Comerford. It turns out bright green, which could explain why Sasha reportedly didn't like it. The secret to the texture could be putting some of the spinach in a blender. This recipe is slightly adapted from the White House version.

2 pounds baby spinach
4 shallots
2 garlic cloves
2 tablespoons olive oil
Salt and freshly ground
** pepper**

1. Wash and clean the spinach. Peel and mince the shallots. Peel and mince the garlic. Place a large bowl of water near the sink, and put a few ice cubes in it. Place a colander in the sink.

2. Fill a medium-sized pot with water. Sprinkle in some salt. Place it on the stove and bring it to a boil over high heat. Carefully add ½ pound of the spinach (about ¼ of the leaves) to the water and let it boil for just 30 seconds to 1 minute (this is called blanching). The leaves will turn bright green!

3. Carefully pour the spinach and water into the colander to drain the spinach. Then immediately "shock" the spinach by putting it right into the ice water. Use tongs or a fork to handle the spinach---it will be hot. Let the spinach sit in the water for a minute or so, then drain it again in the colander. Squeeze the spinach with your hands or press the spinach against the colander with the back of a spoon to remove the excess water.

4. Place the spinach in a blender and puree. Set aside.

5. In a large skillet over medium heat, heat the oil. Add the shallots and garlic, and cook until the shallots no longer look white.

6. Add the rest of the spinach leaves. Toss them with a spoon and sauté until the leaves are wilted. Add the pureed spinach and stir. Season with salt and pepper.

This recipe from Texas is also written in Spanish because Spanish is the first language of many of the young chefs who devised it.

1 whole wheat or corn tortilla

1-2 tablespoons fat-free cream cheese

3 tablespoons chopped spinach, fresh or steamed*

2 tablespoons shredded carrot

1 tablespoon chopped fresh parsley**

1 tablespoon chopped fresh tomato

Note:* You may add any leafy green, broccoli, potatoes or radishes.** You could use cilantro, dill and mint.

1. Place the tortilla on a plate. Spread the cream cheese over the surface.
2. Arrange the spinach, carrot, parsley and tomato on the cream cheese. If necessary, lightly press the vegetables with the back of a spoon so they stick to the cream cheese and don't fall out of the bottom of the tortilla. Roll up the tortilla and eat it right away, or warm it slightly by placing it on a plate, putting it in the microwave, and heating on high for 15-30 seconds.

— Sustainable Food Center's program, The Happy Kitchen / La Cocina Alegre ™

1 tortilla de maíz o trigo integral

1-2 cucharadas de queso crema sin grasa

3 cucharadas de espinacas, frescas o al vapor* (ver nota)

2 cucharadas de zanahoria rallada

1 cucharada de perejil fresco picado **

1 cucharada de tomate fresco picado en cubitos

Nota:* Según gusto y disponibilidad, se pueden utilizar otras verduras de la primavera como arrúgala, espárragos, remolachas, coles de Bruselas, col/repollo, coliflor, acelgas, hojas de mostaza, puerros, lechuga, papas, y champiñones.
**u otras hierbas de la primavera como cilantro, eneldo, y menta

1. Unte el queso crema sobre la tortilla.
2. Coloque la espinaca, la zanahoria, y el perejil, sobre el queso crema.
3. Enrolle la tortilla y disfrute. Una vez enrollada, se puede calentar en el microondas usando su potencia máxima para 15-30 segundos.

Whatever language you speak, you'll enjoy these rolled snacks.

ONIONS

If I told you that a white or red or yellow onion was really an undeveloped clump of leaves from the onion plants, you might not want to believe me. One form of onion green even has a purple flower. Whatever the color, the onion actually packs a lot of flavor for a low-calorie count, which is one reason the White House chef Sam Kass had contestants on "The Biggest Loser" harvest them from the kitchen garden for mega salad (see recipe on p. 24).

This clever recipe from the Dakotas wraps onions in individual foil packages so they can cook on the grill as you make other food. If you don't have a grill or it's freezing outside, you can bake them in the oven. The onion makes its own sauce as it cooks, which renders it soft and juicy. You can make as many packets as there are eaters, or more than one for each larger appetite.

Beets, which the President doesn't like, can be cooked the

same way. Cut off the leafy top and the long stem (which looks something like a mouse's tail) of each beet. Wash them, then wrap each one in foil (no butter or bouillon is needed). They can be cooked and unwrapped the same way as the onions.

When the beets are cool enough to handle, remove their tough outer skin by running the faucet in the sink and rubbing the beets underneath the water. Your fingers may turn pink from the juices in the beets, but the messy peel will stay in the sink. Wear clothes that you don't mind staining, just in case any juices splash.

1 onion
1 tablespoon margarine or butter
1 tablespoon bouillon granules (small pieces) or 1 cube bouillon

1. Preheat a grill to medium or preheat the oven to 375 degrees.
2. Peel the onion and cut off the root end and the top. Carefully use a sharp knife to make a small

hole in the top of the onion (this is a good time to ask a grown-up for help), but don't cut the onion all the way through. If you cut a square slot in the top, you can use a spoon to scoop out a small hole.
3. Place the bouillon in the hole, then lay the piece of butter on top.
4. Place the onion on a sheet of aluminum foil. Pull up the sides of the foil to make a package, scrunching it closed at the top. Place on the top rack of a grill or on a baking sheet in the oven. Grill or bake for 45 minutes to 1 hour (the time will vary according to the size of the onion), until the onion is soft and juicy. You can check if the onion is done by using hot mitts to pull the package off the grill or out of the oven. Use a fork to pull open a little of the foil, and gently poke the onion. If the fork goes into the onion and pulls out easily, the onion is done.
5. Use hot mitts again to remove the onion from the grill or oven. Put the foil package into a small bowl (such as a cereal bowl) and let it cool for about 5 minutes before unwrapping the foil. Be careful — there will be lots of juice inside. Pour any juice from the packet over the top of the onion and serve.

---Tiger Post After School Program
Tiger Post Community Education Center
Ipswich, SD

PEAS PLEASE

Archaeological evidence suggests that humans have been eating peas for at least 11,000 years. But that doesn't mean that every President of the United States or First Lady has enjoyed them. When Hillary Clinton, then resident in the White House, was recording a guest appearance on "Sesame Street" in 1993, she said she didn't want to talk about peas because "hardly anyone likes peas." She asked to talk about apples, instead. Then again, not all people are alike. Thomas Jefferson, for one, loved fresh peas and made, among other things, a soup of them. His recipe is on the next page.

Peas from the shell are some of the easiest vegetables to use because they can be eaten plain, or cooked quickly in just a little boiling water. This makes up for the work it takes to remove them from the pods. You have to shell about 12 pods just to get ¼ cup of peas. But once you do, there are a lot of fun things to do with them. The children in Liz Van Brunt's summer kitchen workshop at the Chautauqua Institution in western New York said they like to sprinkle fresh peas in macaroni and cheese. Others said they put peas in stir-fries, or eat them straight out of the pod.

PEAS WITH BUTTER
Per single serving

This is a simple recipe favored by many Denver families that will work with any quantity of peas that you can shell. Of course, the larger your family, the more peas you need but you may also have a shelling crew. For extra flavor, stir chopped fresh herbs, such as mint and parsley, into the peas after they have cooked.

1/2 **cup shelled peas (from about 24 pods)**
1/2 **tablespoon butter**
Salt, to taste

1. Bring a saucepan of water to a boil.
2. While the water is heating, remove the peas from their pods and place them in a bowl.
3. When the water reaches a boil, sprinkle in some salt and the peas. Cook for only 10 to 30 seconds! Quickly drain in a colander set in the sink.
4. Place the peas in a serving bowl. Add a little butter and a sprinkling of salt.
–– The Denver Urban Gardens
Denver, CO

THE PRINCESS AND THE PEA

Shelly Danko-Day

A Grow Pittsburgh gardener shows off a small-but-beautiful example of good taste.

SORREL

The leaf, raw or cooked, tastes best when harvested young before sharpness sets in.

Historians believe that peas were Thomas Jefferson's favorite vegetable, based on his garden log and other records. He planted 23 varieties at his home in Monticello, and used to have a contest with local landowners to see who could bring the first peas of the season to the table. Household recipes from Monticello were collected in books copied by Jefferson's six granddaughters. This recipe for pea soup is adapted from a manuscript left by Virginia Randolph Trist, one of Jefferson's granddaughters. This mildly flavored soup, thickened with egg yolks and roux (a flour-butter mixture), turns a lovely spring-like chartreuse color.

2 1/2 **cups water**
Salt, for the
    cooking water
1 cup green peas
    (fresh or frozen)
1/2 **teaspoon sugar**
1 1/2 **teaspoons**
    chopped fresh
    herbs, such as
    parsley or sorrel,
    plus more for
    optional garnish
1 tablespoon flour
1 tablespoon butter
2 egg yolks
Salt and pepper,
    to taste

1. Put the water into a saucepan. Sprinkle it with salt, and bring the water to a boil over high heat. Carefully add the peas, making sure the water does not splash. Cook for 2-3 minutes (3-4 minutes if using frozen peas), just until they are tender.
2. Turn off the stove and move the pan off the burner. Place a heat-proof bowl next to it. Using a slotted spoon, carefully lift out the peas and put them in the bowl. Save the water in the pot. Use the back of a wooden spoon to mash the peas.
3. Add sugar and chopped herbs to the cooking water, stirring them in.
4. In a small skillet, melt the butter over medium-low heat. Add the flour, and stir it into the butter, making a paste. This is called a roux and it will help thicken the soup. Keep stirring until the paste is well mixed and starts to smell a bit like toast. Keep stirring to let it brown slightly, but do not let it burn. Add this to the cooking water, whisking it in until all lumps are gone.
5. In a bowl, beat the egg yolks with a whisk or a fork until light and bubbly. Whisk them slowly into the pot.
6. Return the pot to the stove over low heat. Add the mashed peas, salt, and pepper, and stir to combine everything. Gently warm the soup before serving. Do not let it boil. Garnish with additional herbs.

SUGAR SNAP PEAS

Sugar snap peas are a variation of snow peas, developed in 1979, when Jimmy Carter was president. While snow peas are flat with teensy little peas inside, sugar-snaps have fat peas inside. These make a great snack because you can eat the entire pod along with the peas.

This is one crop that doesn't mind a frosty night –– and there are lots of those in a New Hampshire spring. When a group of young New Hampshire gardeners grew tired of eating the pods right off the vine, they made up the recipe that follows.

Tip: Chop up everything and line it up near the stove, because the recipe comes together in a hurry. Also, don't be afraid of gnarly fresh ginger. Once you peel off the tough outer skin, you can grate it with a fine-holed grater instead of chopping it.

SUGAR SNAP PEAS WITH GINGER AND GARLIC
Serves 4

2 shallots
1 tablespoon finely chopped fresh ginger
1 garlic clove
3/4 **pound sugar snap peas**
1/2 **cup water**
Salt and pepper, to taste

1. Peel the shallots and cut them into thin slices. Peel and finely chop the garlic clove. Wash the peas and trim the tough ends.
2. In a large skillet, heat the olive oil over medium-high heat until it's hot but not smoking. Add the shallots, ginger and garlic. Sauté, stirring, for 1 minute.
3. Add the peas and sauté, stirring, for 2 more minutes.
4. Add the water and simmer, stirring occasionally, until the peas are a little tender but still a little crunchy (this is called crisp-tender –– you don't want them to get mushy), about 2 minutes.
5. Season with salt and pepper. Toss them once or twice before serving.

–– Kids Can Grow
University of New Hampshire
Cooperative Extension
Dover, NH

GINGER

THE LAST DAYS OF SPRING

WHITE HOUSE KITCHEN GREEN SALAD WITH CARROTS AND HONEY DRESSING
Serves 4

A few days before summer began — June 16, 2009—it was mild enough for t-shirts, and the garden was lush with herbs and vegetables ready to be enjoyed. Bancroft schoolchildren came back to help the First Lady pluck some of what they'd also helped plant. Because the young garden start-up crew would soon go off on summer vacation, the White House had decided on a first harvest celebration.

With a great deal of pride and pleasure, Mrs. Obama and chef Sam Kass led the way to the lettuce, herbs and other vegetables ready for harvest. Mrs. Obama, wearing a white sweater printed with pink flowers, carefully knelt to pick lettuce, which she handed to schoolgirls who were waiting to put it into large bowls. Other pre-teens plucked finger-length green pea pods off their vines. In total, the group harvested 73 pounds of lettuce, 12 pounds of snap peas and one lone cucumber!

Once all the vegetables for the lunch were gathered in bowls, Kass led the way back up the lawn to the White House kitchen, where he and chef Cristeta Comerford helped the fifth-graders make lunch. After washing their hands and putting on tall chef's hats, some kids washed and chopped lettuce for a salad while others dipped pieces of chicken in eggs, flour and bread crumbs to give the chicken a crispy crust when it baked. Still others, including the First Lady, shelled peas for a side dish to go with the chicken and rice.

Before they ate, Mrs. Obama reminded everyone that a big reason she'd started the garden was to help people "make the connection between what we eat and how we feel, and how healthy we are." She also asked how many had started eating more fruits and vegetables. Many kids nodded. She said she hoped that the Bancroft kids would go out and spread the word about the fun of eating garden-fresh food. "I never want you to get too old or too cool to come back and see me in this garden," she said.

Then the feast began, with a menu of salad, baked chicken, brown rice and garden peas. This was followed by cupcakes with white icing, raspberries and blueberries on top. When it comes to dessert, there's usually no place for vegetables—even at the White House garden.

For the first time ever, the White House has beehives on its grounds, so the honey in this recipe is also a White House crop.

1 head lettuce
2 carrots
1/2 of 1 cucumber
1/4 cup vinegar
   (red wine or balsamic)
   or lemon juice
1 teaspoon honey
1 teaspoon mustard
   (optional)
Salt and pepper, to taste
1/3 cup olive or canola oil

1. Wash and chop the lettuce. Place it in a large bowl.
2. Peel the carrots and cucumber. Cut each one into bite-sized pieces. Place in the bowl with the lettuce.
3. In a small bowl place the vinegar, honey, mustard (if using), salt and pepper. Whisk together while slowly pouring the oil into the bowl. Or just combine these ingredients in a container with a tight, leak-proof lid, and shake vigorously.
4. Just before serving, add the dressing to the bowl of lettuce and vegetables, and toss.

Chicken:
1 (approximately 3 pound)
  chicken, cut into pieces
Salt and pepper, as needed
1 cup flour
1 cup bread crumbs
2 eggs

1. Preheat the oven to 400 degrees.
2. Wash the chicken and pat it dry. Lightly sprinkle salt and pepper on all sides of the chicken. Place flour and bread crumbs in separate shallow bowls. In a third bowl, lightly beat the eggs with a fork.
3. Place each piece of chicken in the bowl of flour, moving it around until the chicken is completely covered on all sides. Knock off any extra flour by holding the piece over the bowl and tapping the chicken with a spoon or your other hand.
4. Dip the flour-covered chicken piece in the egg, covering it completely.
5. Finally, roll the chicken in the bread crumbs, covering completely.
6. Place each piece of chicken in an oiled baking dish and put in the oven for approximately 40 minutes. Do not turn the chicken as it bakes. Test to see if it's done by removing the pan with hot mitts, poking the chicken with a fork, and seeing if the juices are clear (they will be pink if the chicken is still not done). Or use a meat thermometer to see if the temperature inside the largest piece of chicken is 180 degrees.

Brown rice:
1 1/2 cups brown rice
3 cups water
1 tablespoon butter or
  olive oil
Salt, to taste

1. Combine the rice and water in a pot. Cover the pot and bring the water to a boil. Reduce heat to low. Cook for approximately 40 minutes or until all water is absorbed.

2. Carefully remove the lid and stir the rice with a fork to fluff it up. Add the olive oil or butter, sprinkle with salt, and stir before serving.

Peas:
1 pound sugar snap peas or 2 pounds of peas in the pod
2 tablespoons vegetable oil
1 clove garlic or 1/4 teaspoon garlic powder
Salt and pepper, to taste

1. Remove peas from the pod (if using shell peas), or clean and rinse the sugar snap peas. Peel and chop the garlic clove.
2. When the chicken and rice are finished cooking, heat a frying pan on medium-high heat. Add the oil and garlic. Just as garlic becomes golden, add the peas and cook until warm, approximately 1-2 minutes. Add salt and pepper, remove from the heat, and serve.

EVERYBODY LOVES A GARDEN

The White House garden attracted admirers from around the world. When the First Lady, Sasha and Malia went to Europe in late June, that first year of the garden, they were flooded with questions. Later on, Michelle would say, "When I travel around the world, no matter where I've gone so far, the first thing world leaders, prime ministers, kings, queens ask me about is the White House garden."

Copycat gardens have been planted. The Bloom 2009 horticultural festival in Dublin exhibited a replica of the White House Garden. In London, Mrs. Obama reportedly inspired Queen Elizabeth II to plant an organic vegetable patch at Buckingham Palace. British Prime Minister Gordon Brown's wife, Sarah, added edible plants to the property at 10 Downing Street.

Closer to Washington, the W. Atlee Burpee & Co. reproduced the White House Garden at Fordhook Farm in Doylestown, PA.

WHITE HOUSE SPRING VEGETABLE GARDEN

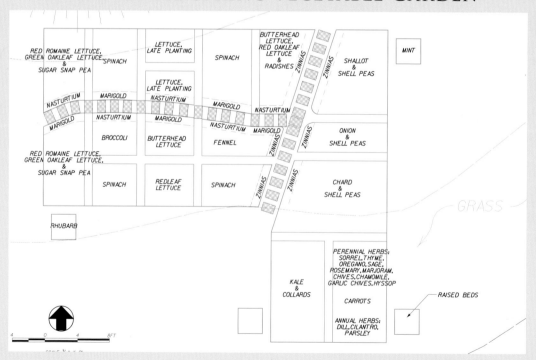

BURPEE REPLICA OF
WHITE HOUSE KITCHEN GARDEN

www.punkrockgardens.com

Burpee CEO George Ball said the replica had been erected in honor of "fellow gardeners" Michelle and Barack Obama. The Burpee garden, like the White House garden, diverged from original plan, heeding soil condition, the weather and the on-the-ground experience. A plan is a plan. A garden is a living thing.

PART III

Summertime
and the Living Is Green

In later June, steady temperatures in the 70s turned the White House Kitchen Garden into a lush, green land-

scape. Lettuce leaves stood as high as chef Sam Kass' ankles, and fennel fronds reached up toward his waist. "So far it's been incred-ible.

We've produced over 200 pounds of food already, going on 210, and it's not even July yet," he said in a video about the garden.

Grounds' crews kept busy weeding the beds and trimming vines that strayed out onto the flat stones that made up the walkway between the garden beds. They didn't need to do much watering, thanks to above-average rainfall all month.

With schools on summer vacation, hordes of tourists began walking past the fence on the south side of the White House, peering in for a better view of the garden. From that distance, the kitchen garden looked like a few clumps of green. The pale blue beehive set on a wooden platform was easier to spot.

The National Park Service installed a plaque near the fence giving a brief history of gardening at the White House, from Thomas Jefferson to Michelle Obama.

THE BOYS OF SUMMER

The first day of summer, which happened to be Father's Day, found Barack Obama, President of the United States, in a white apron with the Presidential Seal on it, standing before a grill on the White House South Lawn. With him was Bobby Flay, Food Network host and cookbook author. The President called Flay "one of the best chefs in the world."

Welcome to the White House First-Day-of-Summer and Happy-Father's-Day Barbecue. Among the guests were actor B.D. Wong, hip-hop artist Darryl McDaniels (the DMC of Run DMC), skateboarder Tony Hawk, basketball pro Dwayne Wade and Vice President Joe Biden. Hawk had warmed up for the barbecue with a brief glide through the White House's Grand Foyer, calling to mind the days when Theodore Roosevelt's six children filled the White House and its grounds with tricycles, bicycles, skates and assorted toys.

President Obama and Flay sprinkled rib-eye steaks with a spice mix — paprika, chili powder, cumin and black pepper. The President described himself as a "medium-well guy," meaning that's how he likes his steaks. The chef said that the steak should only be flipped once as it cooks, which surprised Obama. "You don't take a peek?" he asked.

"You see the edges start to get a little charcoaled on the outside, and that gives you a hint that says, all right, you can flip me now," Flay responded, adding that the steak needed to rest for a few minutes before it was cut so the juices could cool down and redistribute themselves.

Few family cookouts are complete without corn, and this one was no exception. Even if the first White House Kitchen Garden had included corn, it would not have been eye-high ready in June. Corn grown in a warmer climate was the solution. Although almost all the vegetables in this book represent what is grown in the garden, Michelle Obama's goal was not to set an example of food self-sufficiency but to share ideas about healthy growing and eating with other Americans.

On Father's Day at the White House, the President and one of the nation's leading chefs grilled corn that had been blanched first so it would cook faster on the grill. The President and the chef brushed a mixture of melted butter, the garden's gift of fresh basil, chopped small, and garlic on the corn as it cooked. Smoke rose from the White House grill, a scene that was replicated in backyards from Casco Bay to Honolulu as the steak turned that day.

Corn on the cob can be boiled, of course, but grilling adds flavor. By all accounts, the White House grilled corn was simply excellent, but there is also a Mexican twist that might be added to it, as some families who grill together in Tulsa, Oklahoma, know. Below is a recipe that Michelle Obama, who favors Mexican food, should try. And so should you if you like a bit of heat on Americans' favorite native food.

This recipe was submitted by two Tulsa boys, David Pineda and Reece Campos, and comes from David's family. "This is amazing!" the boys wrote in a box surrounded by red dots at the bottom of their carefully handwritten instructions. The Oklahoma boys are right.

Tips: To make the butter easier to spread, take it out of the refrigerator while the corn soaks. Also, to add extra flavors, sprinkle the cooked corn with lime juice and finely grated Parmesan cheese, or the Mexican cotija cheese, if you can find it.

4 fresh ears corn, with husks still on
1/2 cup (1 stick) butter
Chili powder and salt, to taste

CORN

1. Put the corn in a bowl of water, submerging it, and let it soak for 1 hour.
2. Preheat a grill to high heat.
3. Take the corn out of the water. Pull the husk halfway off each one. Spread the kernels of each one with butter. (Save about 1 tablespoon of butter for the rest of the recipe). Pull the husks back up. They should stay in place because they stick to the butter.
4. Tear off four pieces of aluminum foil and spread each one with a little of the remaining butter. Wrap each individual ear of corn in foil.
5. Place the foil packages on the grill. Cook for 15-20 minutes.
6. Take the eloté off the grill and peel off the foil.
7. Pull off the husks and sprinkle each ear of corn with chili powder and salt.

— Global Gardens
Rosa Parks Summer Program
Tulsa, OK

LUAU ON THE LAWN

A few days after Father's Day, the Obamas hosted the Congressional Picnic on the South Lawn. The picnic is an annual presidential tradition dedicated to fun. Jimmy and Rosalyn Carter's 1977 picnic boasted square dancing and clog-dancing performances. George and Laura Bush's 2007 picnic featured horse-and-buggy rides around the White House grounds. Michelle and Barack Obama, harking back to the President's childhood state, held the White House's first luau or Hawaiian outdoor feast.

The Obamas invited Alan Wong, who owns a restaurant in Honolulu and is a big promoter of Hawaiian food, to be the guest chef for the picnic. The hosts specifically requested vats of wasabi potato salad (flavored with horseradish paste) and hoisin baby-back ribs (flavored with Chinese hoisin sauce). The potato, like corn, is a New World native. Hawaiian cuisine melds stateside favorites with Asian flavors and Pacific island specialties. Also on the menu were traditional Hawaiian lomi lomi salmon and kalua pig.

The White House and Wong went international for the desserts: strawberry tiramisu and chocolate bars. The First Family and many of their guests wore leis made of fresh flowers. Hula dancers entertained the more than 2,000 guests.

8 medium potatoes
(about 2 2/3 pounds)
8 slices bacon (optional)
2 cups mayonnaise
2 tablespoons
   prepared white horseradish
1 to 2 tablespoons wasabi paste
   (Japanese-style horseradish)
1 tablespoon Dijon-style
   mustard
1 1/2 teaspoons salt
1/2 teaspoon pepper
1/4 cup finely chopped celery
1/4 cup finely chopped onion
2 tablespoons snipped chives
2 tablespoons finely chopped
   parsley

1. Cut the potatoes into 1-inch pieces. In medium saucepan, add potatoes to 2 inches boiling salted water. Return to a boil; reduce heat to medium. Cook, covered, about 12 minutes or until tender; drain and cool.
2. If using bacon, fry it until crisp. Drain the bacon on paper towels; reserve the pan drippings. Cut bacon into small pieces and set aside.
3. In a large bowl, combine the mayonnaise, 1/4 cup of the reserved bacon drippings (if using), the horseradish, wasabi, mustard, salt and pepper until blended. Add the potatoes, bacon (optional), celery, onion, chives and parsley, tossing carefully until combined. Cover and refrigerate until ready to serve.

Note: Wasabi paste can be found in the Asian food section of some supermarkets. If you can't find it, an additional tablespoon of prepared horseradish may be substituted for the wasabi paste.

— Obama Foodorama Blog

POTATOES

By early July, the garden had yielded more than 225 pounds of produce, some of which was donated to Miriam's Kitchen, a Washington soup kitchen that serves meals to the city's homeless. Beans, eggplant and cucumber would soon be in season. The Bancroft School students were on summer vacation but the White House found extra hands at Brainfood, a culinary training program for high school students in D.C. Brainfood teenagers were invited to help in the White House kitchen and in the garden if they were so inclined. Were they ever! Their eagerness was a good thing, because 1,200 hungry people had been invited to join the First Family on the Fourth of July.

You may have learned in school that George Washington was first in war and first in peace, but you may not know that he also was the first president to host an Independence Day party in 1790, at his official residence in New York City. The White House had not yet been built, and the land that became its lawn and, centuries later, its kitchen garden, was still swamp.

In 1801, the author of the Declaration of Independence and our third President, Thomas Jefferson, held the first Fourth of July reception at the White House. He also reviewed military parades and bands on the holiday. By the 1840s, the White House Fourth of July guest list included local Sunday School students. In 1848, James K. Polk left the grounds of the White House on Independence Day to attend the laying of the cornerstone for the Washington Monument. President Abraham Lincoln, in the middle of the Civil War, used a Fourth of July White House reception to honor soldiers. Later presidents often spent the holiday traveling or attending public ceremonies outside of Washington.

The Obamas had invited military servicemen and women and their families for a barbecue. Red-white-and-blue bunting draped the south portico of the White House as the President and his family, along with Armed Forces special heroes, welcomed the crowd. Daughter Malia, who turned 11 that day, had an American flag painted on one cheek.

At tables surrounded by white chairs and set with blue or red tablecloths, White House chefs dished out an all-American menu: grilled hamburgers and hot dogs, potato salad, watermelon, corn on the cob, garden salad with walnuts and cheese, and ice cream. This was the time for Michelle Obama to relax and enjoy the picnic fare. "There's nothing that the First Family loves more than a good burger," she has said. Like many of us, she admitted to a fondness for French fries. "I love them. Dearly. Deeply. I have a good relationship with French fries and I would eat them every single day if I could." The message? One can't live by healthy fruits and vegetables alone! But one shouldn't live on fried food, either.

Americans have long loved informal food, but for a long time White House occupants thought important guests might be insulted if they served it. In 1939, Eleanor Roosevelt was criticized for serving the visiting English Queen Elizabeth and King George a picnic that included hot dogs, smoked turkey, cranberry jelly, green salad, and strawberry shortcake. Perhaps the less formal setting at their home in Hyde Park made them willing to take the risk. Apparently, the King and Queen were charmed.

Ronald Reagan was better known for his favorite candy — jelly beans — than for more sumptuous fare. During his administration, he was also widely ridiculed for a proposal to classify ketchup as a vegetable in school lunches. This hearty soup, which we have adapted, would have fit right into one of the western movies in which he had acted. It also contains real vegetables, making it something that Mrs. Obama could praise.

1 tablespoon butter or margarine
1 pound lean ground beef
1 clove chopped garlic
1 cup diced onions
3/4 cup sliced carrots
1 cup sliced celery
1/2 cup diced green pepper
6 cups beef broth, beef stock, or water with 4 beef bouillon cubes
8 ounces (1 cup) diced tomatoes (fresh or canned, including the juice)
1/8 teaspoon freshly ground black pepper
5 ounces canned hominy, drained

1. In a soup pot, melt the butter. Add the ground beef and cook, stirring, until it browns.
2. Peel and chop the garlic. Add the onions, garlic, carrots, celery and green pepper. Cover the pot and simmer 10 minutes.
3. Add the beef broth, stock or water with bouillon cubes, along with the tomatoes and pepper. Bring to a boil, then reduce the heat, and let the soup simmer for 35 minutes.
4. Stir in the drained hominy. Simmer for 10 minutes more.

CELERY

PRESIDENTS SCREAM FOR ICE CREAM

PINK ICE CREAM WITH A GLORIOUS PAST

RASPBERRY ICE CREAM
Serves 10

While serving as our new country's ambassador to France, Thomas Jefferson discovered a gastronomical world that included ice cream. He may have introduced the treat to Martha and George Washington. We do know there were two ice cream makers in their household inventory.

A few years later, a free black woman named Sallie Shadd, who owned a Wilmington, Delaware, tearoom, successfully experimented with adding berries to vanilla ice cream. Dolly Madison invited her to make the treat at the White House for an inaugural party for her husband, James Madison. A guest at the party celebrating James Madison's second term wrote about the wonderful pink ice cream he'd enjoyed. Its luscious pink was matched by the dress Dolly wore.

Following is an updated version of Jefferson's 1784 recipe for egg yolk-rich French ice cream, with the addition of fresh raspberries, one of the White House garden fruits. (You can also use strawberries, which is what Sallie Shad did.)

1 cup milk
1 cup heavy cream
1 vanilla pod, split
4 egg yolks
1/2 cup sugar
8 ounces fresh
    raspberries
2 tablespoons
    powdered sugar

1. In a medium saucepan, add the milk, heavy cream, and vanilla pod. Heat slowly to just below boiling.
2. In a bowl using an electric mixer or a whisk, beat the egg yolks with the sugar until thick.
3. Remove the vanilla pod from saucepan and scrape the seeds into the liquid. Pour the liquid into the egg yolk-sugar mixture and stir to combine.
4. Pour the mixture back into the pan and heat slowly to just below boiling, stirring until mixture thickens.

Remove from the heat and allow to cool.
5. When cold, pour into an electric ice cream maker and freeze according to the manufacturer's instructions.
6. Mash the raspberries and strain through a sieve into a bowl. Stir the powdered sugar into the strained berries. A few minutes before the end of freezing in the ice cream maker, swirl in the raspberry sauce through the slot in the machine. Spoon into an airtight plastic container and place in freezer for at least an hour before serving.

— Michael Turback,
author of *A Month of Sundaes*
(Red Rock Press)

MIDSUMMER GARDEN MADNESS

BEANS

Beans and squash grow beautifully throughout the Americas — these hardy New World vegetables gave American Indians many of the vitamins they needed.

The original Americans planted beans with squash and corn, and called them the Three Sisters. These three plants complement each other. The roots of the beans provide nitrogen to the soil, which fertilizes the corn. The tall corn plants provide shade for the squashes.

Though the first White House kitchen garden did not include corn or squash, its planters sowed seeds or put in seedlings for several types of beans, both familiar ones and heirloom varieties. The rarer beans were started with gifts from the Thomas Jefferson estate, Monticello, descendants of vegetables planted there under Jefferson's direction. Agriculture was a topic that greatly interested this founding father. He studied it and wrote of it, using his own grounds as his lab. At the White House in July of 2009, the scarlet runner beans in Thomas Jefferson's plot bloomed with reddish-orange flowers that looked like sparks. Later in summer, caseknife pole beans yielded flat pods shaped like butter knives.

Outside of the Jefferson plot grew the more familiar variety of beans in long, green pods, which were ready to eat in July and kept coming until continued hot weather wilted them.

Monticello/photograph by Skip Jones

These rare scarlet runner beans grow in the Jefferson bed of the White House Kitchen Garden, by grace of seeds from the vast vegetable garden of Monticello.

Michelle Obama has frequently observed that kids are interested in eating vegetables that they have had a hand in growing. This principle has appeal for enterprising families lucky enough to have space for a small garden plot, and after-work and after-school hours to tend it. Resistance to eating vegetables can be overcome if it becomes part of an interesting, fun venture. Some early education planners have reached the same decision, as we've seen.

Another example comes to us from New Hampshire where dietician Karrie Kalich and educators Dottie Bauer and Deirdre McPartlin have made vegetables integral to a preschool curriculum. Realizing that young children are eager to touch, smell and taste everything around them, they came up with interesting ways to use six colorful vegetables, among them green beans. In one classroom activity, children touch the outside of the bean pod, and guess what might fit inside. (A ladybug? A stick? A paper clip?)

This recipe has gone from the preschool classroom to the family kitchen and dining area. Even young kids can help wash the beans and snap off their stems.

GREEN BEAN AND ORANGE PASTA SALAD
Serves 6

1/2 **pound green beans**
3 **carrots**
1/2 **pound whole wheat pasta**
1 **tablespoon balsamic vinegar**
1 1/2 **tablespoons olive oil**
1/2 **cup shredded Parmesan cheese**
Salt and pepper, to taste

1. Bring a pot of water to boil for the pasta.
2. Wash the green beans and snap off the stems.
3. Cut or break the green beans into bite-sized pieces and place them in a steamer or a skillet filled with ¾ inch of water.
4. Steam or cook the green beans over high heat for 5 to 8 minutes or until tender. Cool the beans by rinsing them under cold water.
5. Wash and peel the carrots.
6. Shred the carrots in a food processor or dice them.
7. When the water is boiling, add the pasta and cook for approximately 10 minutes, until al dente (firm but not mushy). When the pasta is done, drain it in a colander. Rinse the colander of pasta under cold water.
8. In a large bowl, combine the vinegar, oil, cheese, salt, and pepper. Add the pasta, carrots, and green beans. Mix until combined.
9. Serve immediately or store in a refrigerator for 30 minutes to cool. If you're planning to store the pasta salad longer, wait to add the vinegar and oil until just before serving. Otherwise the pasta will absorb all the dressing.

— *Early Sprouts: Cultivating Healthy Food Choices in Young Children* by Karrie Kalich, Dottie Bauer, and Deirdre McPartlin (Redleafpress) www.redleaf.org

Even pre-K kids get into cooking in New Orleans. A teacher inspired a class by reading to them the children's classic, **Stone Soup**. From that, the kids became excited about the idea that many things can go into a soup, and even little kids can invent a recipe. When it was time to cook, the children and grown-ups tramped into their thriving school garden in the city's historic French Quarter. The garden was started as a hopeful gesture when the school opened after Hurricane Katrina.

Various vegetables were picked and brought to the school kitchen, where a few teachers had also brought in greens, herbs and spices from home. The kids helped cut everything that needed cutting, then took turns adding ingredients while other students stirred. Creole seasoning also went into the pot.

A Creole blend typically combines onion powder, paprika, garlic powder, celery seed, black pepper, cayenne pepper, and dried herbs such as thyme and oregano. Look for it in the spice section of your supermarket.

CREOLE VEGETABLE SOUP
Serves 10-12

1 clove garlic
1 large onion
1 potato
1 bell pepper
1 cup green beans
3 medium tomatoes
16 ounces
  mushrooms
Approximately 2
  tablespoons extra
  virgin olive oil
1 bay leaf
1 cup dried field peas
  (or any dried pea or
  bean of your choice)
1 tablespoon Creole
  seasoning (Italian
  seasoning blend can
  be substituted), or
  to taste
Salt and pepper, to
  taste
1/2 cup chopped
  fresh basil
3-4 sprigs fresh
  rosemary
4 cups vegetable stock
2 cups water
1 cup sliced carrots
1 (16 ounce) bag
  frozen corn

1. Peel and mince the garlic. Peel the onion and potato, wash the bell peppers and remove the seeds, and rinse the green beans, tomatoes and mushrooms. Cut each vegetable into bite-sized pieces and place each one in a separate container.
2. Place a large soup pot on the stove and heat it on medium-high heat. When the pot is hot, add enough olive oil to coat the bottom. When the oil is hot, add the onion and bell pepper. Sauté, stirring, until the onion begins to soften, about 3 minutes.
3. Add the garlic, bay leaf, Creole seasoning, field peas, salt and pepper. Sauté until the onion is translucent and the bell pepper is soft and tender, about 5 minutes.
4. Add the basil and rosemary, then the stock and water. Stir to combine everything.
5. Add the remaining vegetables: Potato, green beans, tomato, mushrooms, carrots and corn.
6. Bring the soup to a boil then reduce the heat to low and let the soup simmer for about 1½ hours, until the vegetables are tender. You could also make it in a slow cooker, letting it simmer for 4-6 hours. Remove the rosemary sprigs and bay leaf before serving.

— KIPP: McDonogh 15 School
for the Creative Arts
New Orleans, LA

Kipp McDonogh 15 School for the Creative Arts

Inspired by Stone Soup, *two New Orleans pre-K students created their own version, starting with vegetable stock, adding garden vegetables and favorite local spices.*

EGGPLANT

The eggplant is native to India. Europeans used to call the eggplant a "mad apple" because they thought it contained a poison that would drive people insane. Now it's a delicacy in France and England. The English use the French word for this vegetable, *aubergine*, which makes this brownish purple bulbous vegetable sound elegant. Our word, eggplant, comes from the white-skinned version of the vegetable, which does look a bit like a big egg. Far more familiar to most of us are the pear-shaped, purple-skinned varieties. The White House grew the longer, thinner Asian variety, with skin that is tender enough not to require peeling before cooking.

HERBED BABY EGGPLANT
Serves 6

Eggplants combine with another summer favorite, basil, in this recipe. It's one of many family-friendly preparations gathered by Emily Jackson, who started a gardening program in her third-grade classroom and now directs Growing Minds, a part of the national Farm to School Network.

The program trains cooks to go into classrooms in western North Carolina, and also encourages students to write, then write some more. "The garden has made me more interested in fruit and vegetables. I used to hate working in the garden but now I know what I am doing and it is not that bad. It takes responsibility to work in the garden. Because if you weren't responsible the plants would die," wrote one fifth-grader.

3 pounds small Asian eggplants or ordinary pear-shaped purples
3 teaspoons salt
2 teaspoons minced garlic
1/2 cup olive oil
1/3 cup red wine vinegar
Freshly ground black pepper, to taste
1/2 cup fresh basil leaves

1. Remove the eggplant caps and cut each eggplant lengthwise into four pieces. Sprinkle with salt, place in a colander in the sink and let drain 30 minutes. Rinse and pat dry.
2. On a baking sheet, spread the eggplant pieces in a single layer, cut sides up.
3. In a bowl, mix the garlic and oil, and drizzle over eggplants. Bake 30 minutes, until the eggplant is brown and tender. Cool slightly.
4. Cut the basil into thin strips. Place the eggplants in a large bowl, drizzle with vinegar, sprinkle with pepper, add the basil, and toss together.

— Growing Minds
Appalachian Sustainable Agriculture Project
Asheville, NC

The Garden of the World in Sioux Falls, South Dakota, has an international culinary agenda. Most of the children who tend it are immigrants from varied countries, and their tastes reflect this.

In each section of the garden, vegetables from a different part of the world are raised. This recipe was brought in by an Afghani mom.

3 medium eggplants
Salt, as needed
Vegetable oil, as needed
2 medium onions
2 large, ripe tomatoes
1/4 cup water
1 cup tomato sauce
1/4 teaspoon ground coriander
1/4 teaspoon black pepper
1/4 teaspoon turmeric
1 1/2 cups lebany (extra-thick, strained yogurt) or plain yogurt, preferably Greek style
2 cloves garlic
Crushed fresh mint

BOURANEE BAUNJAN (AFGHAN EGGPLANT WITH YOGURT SAUCE)
Serves 6

1. Cut the stems from the eggplants and remove the peel. Cut into round slices approximately ½-inch thick. Place the slices in a colander set in a sink, and sprinkle liberally with salt. Leave for 30 minutes, then rinse and pat dry with paper towels.
2. Add enough oil to cover the bottom of a skillet. Add the eggplant slices in a single layer, and fry until lightly browned on each side, about 4-5 minutes per side. You may need to work in several batches, adding more oil to the skillet as it becomes dry. Set aside the slices on a plate lined with paper towels. As an alternative to frying, preheat the oven to 450 degrees. Place the eggplant slices in a single layer on one or two cookie sheets. Brush each slice with oil on both sides. Bake for 15 minutes. Turn the slices over and bake for 10 to 15 minutes more, until the eggplant is soft and brown. Remove from the oven.
3. Set the oven to 350 degrees.
4. Peel the onions and cut them into thin slices. If the skillet looks dry, add more oil, coating the bottom. Add the onions to the skillet, and sauté until translucent, 8-10 minutes.
5. Slice the tomatoes about ½-inch thick. In a large baking dish, place the eggplant slices in a single layer. Top each one with some sautéed onions, followed by a tomato slice.
6. To the skillet, add the water, tomato sauce, coriander, pepper and turmeric, and salt to taste. Stir together and pour over the layered eggplants. Cover the dish with a lid or aluminum foil and bake for 20 minutes. Uncover the dish and bake 10 minutes more. If the sauce still looks runny, let it bake 5-10 minutes more.
7. While the eggplant is baking, peel and mince the garlic cloves. In a bowl, combine the lebany or yogurt, garlic, and salt to taste.
8. To serve, spread a little of the yogurt mixture on the bottom of a plate. Use a spoon or a spatula to carefully transfer one of the layered eggplants to the plate, placing it on top of the yogurt. Spoon a little more of the yogurt mixture on top, and add a few crushed mint leaves. Serve with pita bread.

— Garden of the World
Multi-Cultural Center of Sioux Falls
Sioux Falls, SD

THAI STYLE CONFETTI CRUNCH CUCUMBER SALAD
Makes 3-4 cups

CUCUMBER

Cucumber plants tend to spread sideways, and the ripe, green vegetables sometimes hide so well under the leaves that it's hard to spot them. Since they are more than 90 percent water, they have a mild flavor but a refreshing crunch. Some types of cucumbers are cultivated to be "burpless"—— that is, not to make you burp after you eat them! The White House Kitchen Garden was rich in cucumbers. Cucumbers were sliced into many White House lunch and dinner salads during the first garden summer —— and the tradition continues.

President Ulysses S. Grant had a different idea about when to eat cucumbers. He liked a cucumber soaked in vinegar for breakfast!

This is a great dish for introducing kids to fresh salads. "The dressing is sweet, the colors are bright, and the peanuts add a familiar favorite flavor," said Rebecca Wheeler, chef, cooking instructor and leader of ethnic market tours in Chicago. Her own children, Julia, 5, and Mack, 3, are not yet interested in many raw vegetables or salads, but "they are happy to help me stir anything I am making," she said.

Students at Hatch Elementary School in Oak Park, Illinois were more receptive to her demonstration, she recalled. "The kids really enjoyed using the back of a spoon to scrape out the cucumber seeds. They seemed surprised by how much they liked the salad, and they gobbled it all up."

Adventurous eaters can accent the cucumbers with a chopped serrano or jalapeno chili pepper.

1 cup distilled white vinegar
1 cup sugar
1 teaspoon salt
1 large cucumber
1 small red pepper
1 carrot
1/2 cup cherry tomato halves
1/2 cup finely chopped roasted unsalted peanuts
1/2 cup loosely packed chopped cilantro leaves and stems

1. In a small saucepan over medium heat, combine the vinegar, sugar, and salt. Bring the mixture to a boil, stirring to dissolve the sugar and salt. Cook for 1 minute at a gentle boil, stirring occasionally. Remove from the heat and cool to room temperature.
2. When ready to serve, peel the cucumber and cut in half lengthwise. Scrape out the seeds with a spoon. Cut crosswise into slices. Dice the red pepper and remove the seeds. Grate or finely slice the carrot. Place the cucumber, red pepper, carrot, cherry tomatoes, peanuts and cilantro in a mixing bowl. Pour the cooled vinegar dressing over the salad ingredients and mix gently. Serve cold or at room temperature.
— Rebecca Wheeler, Chicago, IL

CUCUMBER RAITA
Makes 2-3 cups

1 large or 2 small
   cucumbers
1/2 medium onion
1 clove garlic
1 cup plain yogurt,
   preferably Greek
   style
Large pinch of salt
   and pepper
Juice from 1/4 lemon
1 tablespoon olive oil
3-4 tablespoons
   chopped fresh
   herbs, such as basil,
   chives, oregano,
   mint or dill

1. Peel the cucumber. Remove the seeds and dice it. Peel and dice the onion. Peel and mince the garlic. Place all these vegetables in a mixing bowl.
2. To the bowl, add the yogurt, salt and pepper, lemon juice, olive oil and herbs. Mix all ingredients together.
3. Cover the bowl, put it in the refrigerator, and chill for 30-60 minutes. Serve with pita chips, crackers, fresh vegetables or sliced baguettes.

— The Community Design Center of
Minnesota Garden Corps
Saint Paul, MN

Yogurt-based raita helps neutralize the heat of the peppers, and is on most Indian menus.

The raita recipe here comes from a Minnesota garden group, composed of teens of various ethnicities who also managed farm stands.

MINNESOTA LADIES AMONG THE LEEKS

These teens are hilling up leeks — piling dirt around the bulbous base of a plant to keep it white as the upper leaves turn green.

SHALLOTS

The shallot is named after a city in ancient Palestine, but shallots have long since migrated around the world. This member of the onion family looks something like an overgrown garlic clove, and has a milder flavor than regular onions.

It's a good thing that the rainy spring in Washington did not ruin the crop, since it likes dry soil as it matures. The gardeners at the White House knew they were ready to harvest when the leaves turned yellow.

Laura and George W. must have preferred a mild guacamole, or at least have known it was smart to play it flavorful but safe when cooking for a crowd. Most guacamole recipes use onions but this one employs shallots. Relative mildness is also often a good idea when cooking for a family that includes young children. This recipe makes enough for a summer party, so cut the recipe in half if you're serving a smaller group.

7 shallots
1 jalapeno pepper
8 ripe avocados
1/2 cup finely chopped cilantro leaves (or to taste)
Juice of 4 lemons
1 teaspoon pepper
1 tablespoon salt

1. Peel the shallots and chop them into small pieces. Wash the pepper, remove the seeds, and chop it into small pieces.
2. Cut the avocadoes in half and remove the pits. Scoop the flesh into a bowl. Mash until you like the consistency (you probably want to leave a few chunks for texture), then add the chopped shallots, pepper, cilantro, lemon juice, salt and pepper. Stir until well mixed.
3. Cover with plastic wrap and refrigerate for about an hour before serving. Serve with tortilla chips.

TOMATOES

Tomatoes, native to South America, were not known in Europe until explorers brought them back to Spain in the 1500s. Many Europeans, including Italians, thought they were poisonous, since they belong to the botanical family of nightshade, which includes tobacco as well as belladonna — nicknamed "deadly nightshade" because it is!

Thomas Jefferson grew tomatoes, but most Americans did not eat them raw and preferred them in ketchup — which back then was a name for any prepared condiment used to pep up dinners. Ketchups may have differed as widely as the many home kitchens in which they were jarred.

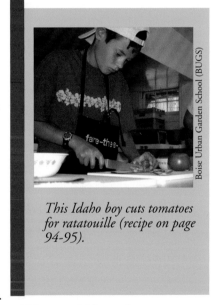

This Idaho boy cuts tomatoes for ratatouille (recipe on page 94-95).

Only around the turn of the 20th century, did tomatoes become more popular. They are botanically a fruit, but are sold as a vegetable. Some gardeners are trying to preserve the older, "heirloom" varieties, which are quirkier and are supposed to have a better flavor than commercially-grown standardized tomatoes.

One of the students at the Bancroft School who helped the First Lady plant other vegetables in April is nevertheless a big tomato fan. He wrote a school report on tomatoes and read it to Mrs. Obama, who described it this way: "He said, not just that they're both a fruit and a vegetable but that . . . they fight diseases like cancer and heart problems, and that they have a lot of vitamins in them, too." And armed with that knowledge, he declared, 'So the tomato is a fruit and it is now my best friend.' "

Tomatoes *do* contain Vitamin C and lycopene, an anti-oxidant that is supposed to help fight disease.

Most gardeners know the problem of waiting, waiting, waiting for your tomatoes to ripen. Then they're all ripe at once! Staggering planting can help. Making tomato sauces to freeze is another solution. And then there is the possibility (while there's nothing quite like a red, juicy, sun-warmed tomato) for an entirely different tomato taste: Harvest a few before they ripen. Fried green tomatoes are especially popular in the South and the Midwest. They even inspired a 1992 movie, based on *Fried Green Tomatoes at the Whistle Stop Café*, a novel by Fannie Flagg about the friendship of two Alabama women in the 1930s.

Some children like fried green tomatoes, too. Nick, who was in the fifth-grade when he participated in a gardening and nutrition program at Denver Urban Gardens in Colorado, said, "When we pick green tomatoes, we bring them into the class and we make fried green tomatoes. We cut them up into pieces and fry them. We put breading around them."

The following recipe comes to us from a Cleveland program, in which teens learn about growing, harvesting and selling produce at local farmers' markets. The recipe calls for two kinds of bread crumbs: The dry, Italian variety and the Japanese style panko, which are light and extra crispy. The combination creates a good balance, but if you can't find panko, use 1 cup of Italian crumbs.

Serves 4

**3 medium size green tomatoes
   (about 1 pound total)**
1/2 **cup Italian bread crumbs**
1/2 **cup panko (Japanese)
   bread crumbs**
1 **teaspoon dried herbs, such
   as basil, oregano, or parsley,
   optional**
Salt and pepper, to taste
2 **eggs**
1/2 **cup milk, optional**
1 **cup flour**
1/4 **cup olive oil**

1. Cut each tomato into ½-inch thick slices. In a shallow bowl, mix the Italian bread crumbs and panko with the herbs, salt and pepper. In another shallow bowl, beat the eggs. Put the flour and milk, if using, into separate shallow bowls. Line up the bowls of ingredients in this order: milk (optional), flour, eggs, bread crumb mix.
2. Line a large plate or a countertop with paper towels. In a skillet, heat 2 tablespoons of the olive oil over medium heat. Dip each tomato slice in the milk, if using, then the flour, then eggs, then the bread crumb mixture, coating both sides.
3. Gently place half the coated tomato slices in the skillet, arranging them so they are not touching. Fry 4-6 minutes on one side, then flip and fry 4-6 minutes on the

other. When done, both sides should look golden brown. Using a spatula, place the cooked tomato slices on paper towels to drain.

4. Add the remaining oil and fry the second half of the coated tomato slices, then drain the second batch on the paper towels.

5. Season to taste with salt and pepper and serve with a knife and fork.

— Cleveland Botanical Gardens
Green Corps
Cleveland, OH

Perfect for a dish of fried green tomatoes

Cleveland Botanical Garden

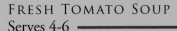

2 stalks celery
1/2 green pepper
1 small onion
1 medium carrot
1/4 cup (4 tablespoons)
   butter or vegetable oil,
   such as canola
5-6 large tomatoes
41/2 cups chicken broth,
   divided
4 teaspoons sugar
1/2 teaspoon curry powder
1/4 teaspoon pepper
1/4 cup flour
About 1/4 cup of chopped
   parsley, for garnish
   (optional)

This soup is like a garden in a bowl, with most of the ingredients harvested by the kids in a South Dakota summer program. This recipe comes from a cookbook that students and parents put together to show everyone their favorite ways to use garden vegetables and herbs.

1. Wash and chop the celery and green pepper. Peel and chop the onion. Peel and shred the carrot. Wash and chop the tomatoes (you should have about 4 cups of tomatoes).
2. In large, heavy saucepan over medium heat, melt the butter or heat the oil. Add the celery, green pepper, onion, and carrot. Continue cooking over medium heat until the vegetables are soft.
3. Add the tomatoes, 4 cups of the chicken broth, sugar, curry powder and pepper. Turn the heat to high and bring the soup to a boil. Reduce the heat to medium or medium-low and simmer, with the pot uncovered, for 20 minutes.
4. In a small bowl, stir together the flour and remaining ½ cup of broth. As you stir the soup, gradually pour in the flour mixture. Continue cooking and stirring until the soup is thick and bubbly. Cook and stir 1 minute more.
5. Remove the soup from the stove (careful, it's hot) and use a ladle to pour some into each serving bowl. Sprinkle a little parsley on each serving, or try another herb, such as fresh basil.

Note: Make your soup more of a main course by sprinkling grated cheddar cheese on top and stirring until it melts in, or make a grilled cheese sandwich to go on the side. If you really want to get creative, make grilled cheese croutons. Make the sandwich the way you usually do, then cut it into bite-sized squares. Float these in the soup.

— Tiger Post After School Program
Tiger Post Community Education Center
Ipswich, SD

GOLDEN LESSONS

Earlier, Brainfood cooking students had visited the White House kitchen and learned to gild pastries for the Obamas' luau.

Another day, they had helped Sam Kass plant Brandywine tomatoes (an old Pennsylvania variety) and Sungold cherry tomatoes, relaxing by plucking mint, and taking pictures with Bo, the First Dog, and garden habitué.

The First Dog, Bo

Jesse Lee/White House Blog

ROASTED TOMATO-GARLIC SAUCE
Serves 4

BRANDYWINE TOMATO

1 sweet onion
5-6 tomatoes (approximately 8 ounces each)
1 head of garlic
About 1/4 cup olive oil
Salt and pepper, to taste

1. Preheat the oven to 400 degrees.
2. Peel and coarsely chop the onion. Remove the stems from the tomatoes and cut them into quarters. Cut the top off the head of garlic, so you can see the tops of cloves.
3. Place all the vegetables in a roasting pan and drizzle with olive oil.

4. Place the pan in the oven and roast until the vegetables are soft enough to puree (about 20 minutes). Remove the pan from the oven.
5. When the vegetables are cool enough to handle, use your clean hands to pop the garlic cloves out of their skins and into the bowl of a food processor or blender. Add the remaining vegetables and puree until well mixed, with a few chunks remaining for texture. Serve with pasta.

— Brainfood
Washington, DC

77

CHAMOMILE
People have drunk this tea since ancient Egypt.

MARJORAM
Closely related to but milder than oregano.

ANISE HYSSOP
Its leaves are brewed for tea but bees prefer its ornamental purple flowers.

As more and more of the herbs that Michelle Obama and her helpers had planted in the spring came up, Sam Kass told MSNBC that the First Family was eating herbs nearly "every night" at their private meals. And why not? The White House grows so many kinds of herbs that at least one of them might complement something on any menu. The list includes Anise hyssop, basil (sweet and Thai), chamomile, chives (regular and garlic chives), cilantro, dill, fennel, oregano, marjoram, mint, rosemary, parsley, sage, sorrel and thyme.

Anise hyssop and chamomile commonly are dried and used for tea. Almost all the other herbs can also be dried for off-season cooking. However, here are ways that some cooks have found to use a few herbs fresh from their gardens.

MINT

Mint grows like a weed (the White House Kitchen gardeners wisely put it in its own bed), but its aromatic leaves can be incomparably refreshing on a sweltering day.

Students at Wonderland Avenue School in Los Angeles brewed tea with a half cup of fresh mint leaves and a quart of boiling water, with agave nectar for sweetening. (Honey or sugar would work just fine, too.) Any self-respecting Southerner knows that fresh mint leaves belong in a glass of iced tea, but a few crushed leaves can liven up lemonade or just plain ice water. Mint also makes the perfect garnish for almost any fruit or dessert as the following recipe shows.

Children in a summer program in Tulsa are especially fond of mint from their summer garden. Garden educator Annie Ferris reported that one student taught the group how to make Vietnamese spring rolls with the fresh mint.

Another invented a "Fresh, Clean Feeling Salad," which left everyone with fresh, minty breath for hours after eating. After Caitlynn Kirsch and Emma Rehn demonstrated and served this fruit salad recipe, Mason, another gardener said, "You know what would make this salad even better? Nothing!"

FRESH CLEAN-FEELING MINTED FRUIT SALAD
Serves 8

1 pint fresh strawberries
3 kiwis
1 cantaloupe
1 pound mixture of red and green grapes
2 apples
4 bananas
1 small watermelon
1 bunch fresh mint

1. Wash all of the fruit and mint.
2. Slice the strawberries and put them in a large bowl.
3. Prepare and put the remaining fruit in the bowl: Peel and slice the kiwis. Dice the cantaloupe. Slice the grapes in half. Cut the apples into squares. Slice the bananas into circles. Cut the watermelon into small pieces.
4. Pull the mint leaves from the stems and cut them into little bits. Add them to the bowl.
5. Toss your salad together and enjoy.

—Global Gardens Rosa Parks Summer Program
Tulsa, OK

Rosa Parks Summer Program

This salad brings together some of the best of the summer harvest — juicy melons, fresh cherry tomatoes, crunchy cucumbers. The surprise twist is Thai basil. The recipe comes from Keith Fuller, executive chef at Six Penn Kitchen in Pittsburgh, who made it with students at the Edible Schoolyard program at Grow Pittsburgh.

Salad:
1/2 **cantaloupe**
1/2 **cucumber**
1-2 **shallots**
3 to 4 cups **cherry tomatoes**
3-4 teaspoons fresh **Thai basil leaves**
Salt and pepper, to taste

Dressing:
3-4 teaspoons **honey**
3-4 teaspoons **balsamic vinegar**
2-3 tablespoons **extra virgin olive oil**

For the salad:
1. Cut the cantaloupe into small chunks. Peel the cucumber, remove the seeds, and dice it. Peel and thinly slice the shallots. Cut each cherry tomato in half. Cut the Thai basil into thin strips (this is called a chiffonade).
2. In a large bowl, gently toss together the cantaloupe, cucumber, tomatoes, basil, and shallots.

For the dressing:
1. Mix the dressing ingredients in a bowl.
2. Pour over the fruit and vegetable mixture. Add salt and pepper to taste. Let it sit for a few minutes to blend the flavors before serving.

— Grow Pittsburgh
Edible Schoolyard Program
Pittsburgh, PA

BASIL

Warm, sunny days bring sweet basil into its full, fragrant, green glory. This herb is essential to Italian cooking, perhaps because it is a tomato's best friend. There's nothing simpler than a salad of fresh tomatoes topped with salt, pepper, extra-virgin olive oil and a few fresh basil leaves. Or toss a bowl of hot pasta with the same ingredients.

The White House also grew Thai basil, a spicy variety, which is closer in flavor to mint or anise than to sweet basil. It would make an exotic garnish for healthy First Family dinners of broiled fish and steamed vegetables.

Most of us think of pesto — a pungent puree of basil, garlic, pine nuts and Parmesan cheese — as a staple of Italian food. It originated in Genoa but is now also popular in the United States. Though it is often tossed with pasta, chef Laurey Masterson discovered a new way to serve it on a day she was planning to teach a group of North Carolina youngster how to make apple tarts. They showed up with apples, and also fresh basil from the garden.

She helped them make the tarts, but while these were baking, she decided to make a quick batch of pesto. "While they liked their tarts, they raved about the pesto," she said. "There were extra, unused apple slices and before I knew it, they had appropriated those apples and devoured the remains of the pesto. At the end, in a show of hands, the pesto ranked up much higher than the tart!"

"I like pesto better than cake!" one child happily proclaimed.

PESTO SAUCE

**1 pound fresh
basil leaves
1/2 cup pine nuts
1/2 cup grated
parmesan cheese
1-2 cloves fresh
garlic (optional)
Approximately 1/4
cup olive oil**

1. In a food processor, add the basil leaves and pulse to break them up.
2. Add the pine nuts, parmesan cheese and garlic. Pulse until just mixed.
3. With the motor of the food processor still on, drizzle in the olive oil through the tube in the top just until a thick paste is achieved. Serve with crackers or apple slices!

— Laurey Matthews
Laury's Catering
Asheville, NC

PIZZA PARTY

Makes 2 large pizzas

When Michelle Obama was growing up, take-out pizza was a special treat. "We had pizza about once every school year — once every semester when we got good grades. That's when we got pizza; it was pizza day," she said.

When gardening groups make their own pizza with fresh vegetables, it's also a treat. Teens at the Community Design Center of Minnesota in St. Paul make an "Everything but the Kitchen Sink" grilled veggie pizza on whole-wheat tortillas. The Tiger Post After School in Ipswich, South Dakota, reinterprets pizza by making it out of refrigerated crescent roll dough, baked, cooled and topped with cream cheese and chopped fresh broccoli, cucumbers and carrots.

In New York state, the governor's executive chef, Noah Sheetz, cooks with as much garden produce as possible. He frequently demonstrates recipes to children that use fresh, local ingredients, including this one for pizza. Do-it-yourselfers make their own cheese with him. Toppings and chopped fresh herbs, including oregano, can be varied according to what's in season (you can even cheat and use commercially prepared tomato sauce), but the crust is a constant, and for good reason. After a notoriously picky 16-year-old took her first bite, she declared, "This is the best crust I have ever tasted!"

Ground Up

People of all ages love to roll out pizza dough

Crust:
1 cup warm water (about 110 degrees)
2 packages active dry yeast
1/4 cup olive oil, plus more for the bowl
2 1/2 cups all-purpose flour, plus more for sprinkling countertop
1/2 cup whole wheat flour
1 1/2 teaspoons salt
2 tablespoons brown sugar

Swiss chard Pesto:
1 pound Swiss chard leaves, center stems removed
1 cup olive oil
1 bunch of basil leaves without stems (about 1 1/2 ounces)
1/2 cup grated parmesan cheese
3 cloves garlic
1 cup pine nuts
1 teaspoon salt
1/4 teaspoon black pepper

Eggplant:
2 small Japanese eggplants or 1 medium eggplant
Olive oil, as needed

Final step:
Olive oil, for the pan
1-2 cups shredded mozzarella cheese
Grated Parmesan cheese, to taste (optional)

For the crust:
1. In a large bowl, whisk together the water, yeast and olive oil. Let stand until the yeast dissolves and starts bubbling.
2. Add both kinds of flour, the salt and sugar.
3. Sprinkle a countertop or another clean work surface with a little flour. Keep more flour next to you to continue sprinkling as needed. Using your clean hands, mix the dough by hand in the bowl until it comes together, then turn it out onto the countertop. Knead the dough about 10 minutes, until it is smooth and elastic, sprinkling it with more flour as it becomes sticky. Or mix the dough in an electric mixer with a bread hook attachment until smooth and elastic.
4. Place 1-2 teaspoons of olive oil in the bottom of a clean mixing bowl. Place the dough in the bowl, immediately turn it over, then cover the bowl with plastic wrap. Let it rise while you prepare the toppings. It should rest for about 1 hour, until it doubles in size.

For the Swiss chard pesto:
1. Bring a pot of water to a boil. Add the basil and chard leaves and blanch for 1 minute.

2. Drain the leaves in a colander and rinse with cold water. Squeeze out the excess water. The greens will clump into a ball, but this is fine.
3. Combine the leaves with the remaining ingredients in a food processor. Blend the pesto until smooth and a little chunky, 3-4 minutes.

For the eggplant:
1. Preheat the oven to 350 degrees. Split the eggplant in half lengthwise and rub the outside with olive oil.
2. Place the eggplant, cut side down, on a baking sheet. Bake for 10 minutes. Let the eggplant cool and then slice into thin half rounds.

For the final step:
1. Set the oven to 450 degrees.
2. Punch down the dough. Divide the dough in half. Lightly grease a large round or square pizza pan with olive oil.
3. Place one batch of the dough on the pan and spread it to the edges. Spread the pesto over the dough and arrange the sliced eggplant on top. Sprinkle the mozzarella cheese evenly over the pizza, adding a little grated Parmesan if desired. Repeat these steps to make a second pizza, or tightly wrap the dough and freeze for another time.
4. Bake for 20 minutes or until the crust is golden brown and the cheese has melted.

— Noah Sheetz
Albany, NY

OREGANO

Because of its strong, almost woodsy flavor, oregano tends to be less popular in kitchens than parsley or basil. Yet the flavors of pizza stand up nicely to it.

The Camden Children's Garden in New Jersey makes room for a big patch of oregano in its Giant Pizza Garden. This section of the garden grows the essentials for topping a pizza (except for the cheese): Basil, oregano, peppers and tomatoes. Families can take special workshops, bringing home seedlings to start a container garden with whatever herbs and vegetables they want to put on their pizzas — their own version of pie in the sky.

CATE'S WHEAT PIZZA CRUST
Makes enough for 4 approximately 8-inch round pizzas

Tip: Pizza dough can be tightly wrapped and frozen for later use. Thaw it before using.

1 package active dry yeast
2 cups warm water (about 110 degrees)
1 tablespoon salt
3 to 3 1/2 cups all-purpose flour
2 cups whole wheat flour
1 teaspoon olive oil

1. Place the yeast in a small bowl. Add ¼ cup of the warm water and stir to dissolve the yeast. Let it sit 5-10 minutes until it begins to bubble.
2. In a large bowl, pour the remaining 1 ¾ cups of warm water and mix with the salt.
3. Add 1 cup of the all-purpose flour and the whole wheat flour, and stir to incorporate. Add the yeast mixture and mix well.
4. In an electric mixer fitted with a dough hook or using a spoon, mix in about 1 cup of the remaining all-purpose flour. Mix until the dough is smooth. Add another ½ to 1 cup of the all-purpose flour to make a soft dough. Let the dough rest for 5 to 10 minutes.
5. Sprinkle flour on a countertop or another clean surface. Place about ½ cup of all-purpose flour in a container next to you. Knead the dough until it is smooth, about 10 minutes, adding more flour as necessary to prevent it from becoming sticky. Alternately, continue to mix the dough in the mixer until smooth and elastic, adding more flour as necessary.
6. Place the oil in the bottom of a large mixing bowl. Add the dough. Cover the top of the bowl with plastic or waxed paper and a clean dish towel. Place it somewhere warm and let it rise until it doubles in size, approximately 2 hours.
7. Punch the dough down and divide it into four equal pieces. Let the pieces rest for 15 minutes then form them into pizza rounds. Add the desired toppings and bake at 500 degrees until golden brown.

— Cate Rigoulot, Camden Children's Garden
Camden, NJ

HAPPY BIRTHDAY, MR. PRESIDENT

On August 5, 2009, his 48th birthday, President Obama personally delivered chocolate cupcakes to another birthday child, reporter Helen Thomas, who had turned 89 that day. If you've ever watched a White House press conference on TV you might have noted Helen as the lady in red.

Later that day, Barack Obama cut into his own chocolate birthday cake, which had a presidential seal on top and was surrounded by a ring of frosting daisies.

Then there were the pies. The President of the United States has described himself as a pie man and White House Pastry Chef Bill Yosses obliged with several flavors — pecan, huckleberry, coconut cream and key lime. (A cheesecake was thrown in for good measure.) Each pie had a candle in the center. Singing "Happy Birthday" to the President and helping him devour the bounty on the table were Sasha and Malia, the First Lady and about 30 White House staffers.

One way to make sweets just a tad healthier is to use recipes that call for fresh fruit. That principle also works for ice cream (see p.63) which, of course, also contains calcium.

BASKETS OF BERRIES

The raspberries, blueberries and blackberries that grew in the White House garden provided the Obamas with summer fruit. Blueberries are native to North America, and were a favorite of American Indians. The huckleberry — which inspired the first name of Mark Twain's famous character — is closely related to the blueberry but it grows primarily in the west. Raspberries and blackberries are bramble plants that grow in America as well as Europe.

As the White House berry patches become more established, the yields should increase each summer.

HUCKLEBERRIES

BLUEBERRIES

This native fruit still grows wild in coastal pockets but was cultivated in the White House garden.

This cobbler, described by Bill Yosses as "one of the First Family's favorites," had been served with caramel ice cream at a White House event early in Barack Obama's first year---the Governors' Ball Dinner on February 22, 2009---when the kitchen garden was still just a gleam in Michelle Obama's eye.

When giving a tour of the White House kitchen with culinary students, Mrs. Obama said that the President calls Yosses "the crust master." She went on to say that the pastry chef makes "the best pies and tarts that come out of this place, and the fillings are just perfection." And that, she good-naturedly continued, "is a problem."

WHITE HOUSE BERRY COBBLER
Serves 6-8

6 tablespoons (3/4 stick) unsalted butter
1 cup all-purpose flour
2 teaspoons baking powder
1/2 teaspoon salt
1/2 teaspoon freshly grated nutmeg
1 cup sugar
2/3 cup milk
2 cups huckleberries or blueberries (about 11 ounces)

1. Preheat the oven to 375 degrees.
2. In an 8-inch square or other 2-quart baking dish, melt the butter. (Use the microwave if it's a glass or other microwave-safe dish; put the pan in the oven for a few minutes if the dish is metal.)
3. In a bowl, sift together the flour, baking powder, salt, and nutmeg. Stir in the sugar until it's well combined.

4. Add the milk and whisk the batter just until it is combined.
5. Pour the batter into the melted butter; do not stir. Pour the berries into the center of the batter. Again, do not stir.
6. Bake the cobbler in the middle of the oven for 40 minutes, or until the cake portion is golden and the berries have given out their juices.

— Obama Foodorama Blog

White House's starter blackberry crop

Clara Silverstein

RASPBERRY

A rose is a rose, and a raspberry is its relative. Eat a raspberry soon after it's picked or it may spoil.

The filling for this cheesecake requires no baking, which makes it an ideal summer treat. The smooth, white surface of the cake is a pristine canvas for the berries, which can be arranged in pinwheels or any number of other patterns, but you need not stop there. You can drizzle the top with melted chocolate, sprinkle it with crushed Heath bars, or even tuck in a few chocolate chips among the berries.

Tip: Make your own graham cracker crumbs in a food processor or by placing the crackers in a sturdy, re-sealable plastic bag, and pressing the bag with a rolling pin.

Crust:
1 cup graham cracker crumbs (from approximately 8 rectangular crackers)
3 tablespoons melted butter
1/2 teaspoon cinnamon
1 tablespoon sugar

Filling:
2 cups blueberries or raspberries, or a combination
8 ounces regular or low-fat cream cheese, softened
1/4 cup plain yogurt
1/4 cup sugar
1 teaspoon vanilla
Milk, if needed
1-2 tablespoons melted chocolate, for garnish (optional)
Fresh mint sprigs, for garnish (optional)

For the crust:
1. Preheat the oven to 350 degrees.
2. In a bowl, mix together the crust ingredients. Transfer the mixture to a 9-inch springform pan (this is a pan with a removable side; if you don't have one, just use a regular 9-inch pie pan). With your clean hands, press the crust into the bottom of the pan, patting it down and pressing it so it is even all around.
3. Bake the crust for 10 minutes, until lightly brown. Let it cool completely before making the filling.

For the filling:
1. Wash the fruit and set it on paper towels to dry.
2. Place the cream cheese, yogurt, sugar and vanilla in a bowl. Using an electric mixer, beat on medium speed for 2 minutes, stopping once to scrape down the sides of the bowl.
3. Stir it with a spoon. It should be about as thick as cake frosting, but not too thick to spread. If it's too thick, stir in a little milk, a teaspoon at a time.
4. Spoon the filling into the prepared crust, gently spreading it with a rubber spatula or a butter knife. Do not press down or work too fast, or crumbs from the crust may break off. Cover the top of the pan with plastic wrap and chill in the refrigerator for 1-2 hours.
5. Just before serving, remove the side of the springform pan and arrange the berries around the surface of the cheesecake. For a decoration, dip a fork into the melted chocolate, and drizzle it over the surface, quickly moving your arm back and forth (don't be too energetic, or you may fling chocolate all over your kitchen). Place a mint sprig in the middle, or a few leaves around the top of the cake.

Not every berry recipe needs to be a dessert. These pancakes are a staple for Melissa Graham, a Chicago chef whose Purple Asparagus programs at farmers' markets and schools encourage good, healthy family meals. She often brings along her son, Thor, 6, as a helper. "Whenever I make this recipe, my son is right at my side, given his love of both blueberries and pancakes. At a Purple Asparagus talk on family eating, he insisted that he come with me. He did a great job until he started licking the measuring spoon we used for the honey," she recalled.

This recipe is ideal for family weekend breakfast. Kids love almost all pancakes and these are sophisticated enough for adults to enjoy.

Note: To make your own buttermilk, see tip on page 35.

1/2 **cup unbleached all-purpose flour**
1/4 **cup buckwheat flour**
1 **teaspoon baking powder**
1/4 **teaspoon kosher salt**
3 **tablespoons unsalted butter**
1/2 **cup buttermilk, well shaken**
2 **tablespoons honey, preferably buckwheat**
1 **large egg**
1/2 **cup blueberries**

1. In a mixing bowl, combine the two kinds of flour, baking powder, and salt.
2. Melt 2 tablespoons of the butter and let it cool slightly. In another bowl, whisk together the buttermilk, honey, egg, and melted butter. Add this to the flour mixture and mix until thoroughly combined.
3. Gently fold in the blueberries.
4. In a skillet or on a griddle over medium heat, melt the remaining tablespoon of butter. Drop approximately ¼ cup of batter onto the griddle to make each pancake. When the thick bubbles pop on the non-griddle side and the pancake is browned, flip and brown the other side. Serve with maple syrup.
— Melissa Graham, Purple Asparagus
Chicago, IL

SOME PLANTS LIKE IT VERY HOT

August heated up in Washington, with 12 days of 90-plus degrees and high humidity that made sitting on a city park bench feel like sitting in a sauna. Members of the Supreme Court were off somewhere doing some deep thinking (or so we hope) and Congress was in recess for most of the month. Other workers who could, took cover in air conditioning, or scurried off for summer vacation. The Obamas went to Martha's Vineyard during the week of August 23.

In the White House garden, however, the plants that like hot weather, especially okra and peppers, were thriving. It's no surprise that both of these plants originally come from warmer parts of the globe — okra from Africa, and peppers from South America. Red tomatoes carried on, peeking through the leaves of lush, green tomato plants, held up by wooden stakes.

One piece of August good news was that earlier bad news — reports that the White House Garden was filled with lead because it had once been fertilized with sludge — was disproved. Word came out that the soil had been tested before the garden was planted, and found to be within acceptable limits. Fertilizers added to the soil had brought down the levels even further.

A tray of just-picked bell peppers at the farmer's market

Clara Silverstein

OKRA

Slave ships probably brought okra from Africa to America. The imported plant thrived in the summer heat of the southeastern states, and okra is still a popular vegetable in the region.

It has long been a White House staple, too. We know that both Thomas Jefferson and James Monroe occasionally dined on okra. *The White House Cookbook, 1894*, published during Grover Cleveland's administration, lists a recipe for boiled okra.

The edible okra pods contain a substance that becomes slimy when cooked, making them an ideal natural thickener for soups and stews. Boiled okra is best sprinkled with a little vinegar, eaten with rice, or both. Perk it up with hot sauce –– something the early presidents probably would not have done.

Avoid using an iron or copper pot to cook okra, as a chemical reaction will turn it black.

OKRA SOUP
Serves 6

3 cloves garlic
1 cup stock — chicken, beef, or seafood
1 habanero pepper, or just a slice because it's super hot
1/2 pound ground beef, chicken, or firm fish fillet, such as cod or tilapia
1 onion
2 tablespoons olive oil
1 pound okra
1 tablespoon dried shrimp (available at a Caribbean or Asian supermarket), optional
1 bunch (approximately 6 ounces) chard, collards, or other fresh greens, cut up into small pieces
Salt, to taste

1. Peel the garlic cloves. Put them in a blender with the stock and pepper. Blend until smooth.
2. If you are using chicken or fish, cut it into bite-sized pieces. Put it in a soup pot and pour the blended mixture over the top. Put it on the stove, turn the burner to high heat, and bring it to a boil. Lower the heat to simmer the soup while you prepare the okra.
3. Peel and chop the onion. Cut the okra pods crosswise into slices about ¼-inch thick. In a skillet, heat the olive oil. Add the onion and cook, stirring, until it softens, about 5 minutes. Add the okra slices and continue to cook, stirring, about 5 minutes more. Do not be surprised when the okra turns gluey.
4. Add the okra and onions to the soup pot. Add the dried shrimp and the chard or collards. Bring the soup to a boil again, then lower the heat to a simmer. Cover the pot and simmer for 15 minutes. Add more water if it looks too thick. Salt before serving.

— Agape Youth Garden
Life Changers Family Community Development
Lanham, MD

In colonial days, gumbo simply meant a stew made with okra, perhaps because the word "gumbo" itself comes from the African word for okra. But by the time the United States was established, or soon after, gumbo recipes from planters' kitchens had expanded to include chicken. Seafood and sausage were not yet in the mix, and gumbo had not yet become associated with New Orleans.

A collection of recipes from Thomas Jefferson's Monticello home includes gumbo made with a quart of okra and a quart of tomatoes, as well as meat (chicken or veal preferred) and onions. Filé powder, made from ground sassafras leaves, could be substituted for the okra, but only after the soup had boiled for 4-5 hours and was off the stove!

This is an adaptation of James Monroe's original jumbo-sized gumbo recipe, which called for two chickens and a half-peck (four quarts) of tomatoes. This recipe is a more manageable size!

1 tablespoon vegetable oil, such as canola
3 slices bacon or turkey bacon
1 large onion
1 chicken (approximately 3 pounds), cut up
Salt and pepper, to taste
2 (15-ounce) cans diced tomatoes
1 cup water
1 1/2 cups approximately 1/2-inch slices of okra (from about 12 pods)
Chopped fresh parsley, for garnish (optional)

1. In a large stainless steel or ceramic pot, heat the oil over medium-high heat. Cut the bacon strips into 1-inch pieces and add to the pot. Sauté the bacon until crispy, 5-6 minutes. Using tongs, remove the bacon to a paper towel-lined plate. Leave about 2 tablespoons of oil in the skillet and discard the rest.

2. Peel and dice the onion, and add it to the pot. Sauté until it begins to brown, 4-5 minutes.
3. Sprinkle the chicken pieces with salt and pepper. Add them to the pot and cook, turning, until they brown all over.
4. Add the bacon back to the pan, along with the tomatoes and water. Bring the mixture to a boil over high heat, then reduce the heat, cover the pot, and let it simmer for 20 minutes.
5. Add the okra, cover the pot again, and let the soup simmer until the okra is tender, approximately 20 minutes. Season to taste with salt and pepper, sprinkle with parsley, and serve.

Note: If the soup looks too thin after the okra is tender, remove the chicken and set it aside in a bowl. Return the mixture to a boil, and let it continue to boil until the liquid is reduced.

PEPPERS POP OUT

BELL PEPPERS

Green bells are peppers that have not yet ripened to yellow, orange or red.

ANAHEIM PEPPERS

These peppers are less hot than other chiles.

Tip: You can make peppers milder by cutting away the ribs and disposing of them and seeds. Don't rub your eyes after handling peppers; the capsaisin is irritating.

Peppers range from sweet bell peppers to habaneros so hot that one morsel can make your eyes water. The White House grew both types of peppers. Among the chilies were the fairly mild banana pepper (which looks like the tropical fruit) and the slightly hotter Anaheim, used for *chili rellenos.*

Capsaicin, the substance that makes some peppers fiery, is concentrated in the ribs and seeds of chilies. The heat in chilies is measured in something called Scoville units, named after Wilbur Scoville, who invented the method in 1912. Bell peppers contain no capsaicin. Anaheim chilies are at the mild end of the scale, while jalapeno peppers are in the middle. Rated as extreme peppers are habañero, Jamaican hot, and Scotch bonnet.

Mark D. Gilbert

The candidate holds up art by a boy who made his chili.

1 large onion
1 green bell pepper
Several cloves of garlic
1 tablespoon olive oil
1 pound ground turkey or beef
1/4 teaspoon ground cumin
1/4 teaspoon ground oregano
1/4 teaspoon ground turmeric
1/4 teaspoon ground basil
1 tablespoon chili powder
3 tablespoons red wine vinegar
Several fresh tomatoes, depending on size (or 1 15 ounce can of diced tomatoes with juice)
1 (15 ounce) can red kidney beans

Tip: I suggest starting with 4 cloves of garlic and 2 cups of chopped fresh tomatoes. You can substitute 1 teaspoon of fresh chopped oregano and 1 teaspoon of fresh chopped basil for those two dried herbs on the ingredient list.

Of course you can adjust everything to taste, including the spices. It's the people's choice!

1. Peel and chop the onion. Wash the pepper, remove the seeds, and chop. Peel and chop the garlic.
2. In a pot over medium heat, heat the olive oil. Add the onion, green pepper, and garlic. Sauté until the vegetables are soft.

3. Add the ground meat and sauté until it browns.
4. In a small bowl, mix together the cumin, oregano, turmeric, basil, and chili powder. Add to the ground meat.
5. Add the red wine vinegar to the pot and stir to combine.
6. Chop the tomatoes and add to the pot. Simmer until the tomatoes cook down.
7. Drain the kidney beans in a colander in the sink and rinse with cold water. Add the beans and cook for a few more minutes.
8. Serve over white or brown rice. Garnish with grated cheddar cheese, onions and sour cream.

Helesa Lahey

Aytan and Leslie Diamond and their two children, Marcus and Zoe, made Obama's warming chili one frigid New York weekend. They went the route of fresh herbs.

The movie "Ratatouille" inspired the children at Boise Urban Garden School (BUGS) to make their own ratatouille, a classic French vegetable stew.

But nothing was that clear at first. "They kept describing a dish that I did not in any way recognize as ratatouille," explains Culinary Program Director Susan Medlin. "There was nothing to do but go see the movie. Once I realized that ratatouille had been raised to haute cuisine, I sat down with students and we devised a way to glam up the always-delicious but humble mélange. This recipe is the result."

The students liked the results so much that they insisted on serving it to the mayor of Boise when he came to do a ribbon cutting at the group's new farm stand, even though he said he could only stay for 10 minutes. He ended up eating lunch with the kids. Maybe it's because the red peppers, green zucchini and brownish-purple eggplants make such a colorful presentation on a platter.

Serves 6-8

Tip: A bouquet garni is a bunch of herbs tied together or bundled together in a piece of cheesecloth, used to flavor a soup or stew. The bag helps with easy removal of the herbs when the dish is cooked.

Bouquet garni:
12 parsley stems
8 peppercorns
2 sprigs thyme
1/4 teaspoon fennel seeds
1 bay leaf

Place the ingredients in a piece of cheesecloth and tie it at one end with clean string or a piece of dental floss.

Ratatouille:
6 tablespoons olive oil, preferably organic
1 pound chopped onions
1 pound red bell pepper
1 pound tomatoes or 1 (15-ounce) can diced tomatoes
1 pound eggplant
1 pound zucchini
Salt, pepper, and balsamic vinegar, to taste
Feta cheese, for serving
1/4 cup chopped fresh parsley

1. In a medium frying pan with a heavy bottom (stainless steel or ceramic works best), heat 2 tablespoons of the olive oil over medium heat. Add the onion and the bouquet garni (the bouquet should be submerged in the onions so its flavors release). Cover the pan and cook, stirring occasionally, until the onions are tender and a light golden color, 8-10 minutes.

2. Cut the peppers into approximately half-inch pieces. Add them to the pot, cover, and cook about 30 minutes more, until the peppers are completely soft.

3. If using fresh tomatoes, cut them in wedges and add them to the pot. If using canned tomatoes, simply open the can and pour them in, juice and all. Cover the pan and cook slowly for another 15 minutes, stirring occasionally. If a lot of liquid has accumulated in the pan, drain it and save it. Uncover the pan and cook until the mixture is quite thick and the liquid has evaporated. Carefully watch the pot, turning down the heat if necessary, and stir so it does not burn. Put this mixture into a heat-proof bowl and set it aside.

4. Peel the eggplant and cut it into approximately half-inch cubes. In the same pan, heat another 2 tablespoons of olive oil. Add the eggplant, cover the pot, and cook until the eggplant is soft, about 20 minutes. Stir occasionally to make sure the eggplant does not stick to the bottom of the pan. Once again, if a lot of liquid has accumulated in the pan, drain and add it to the bowl with the liquid from the tomato/onion mixture. Put the eggplant into a clean bowl.

5. Cut the zucchini into approximately half-inch cubes. Again, in the same pan, heat the remaining 2 tablespoons of olive oil. Add the zucchini. Cover the pan and cook until the zucchini is soft, stirring occasionally, about 20 minutes. If necessary, drain and add the liquid to the bowl containing the liquid from the onions. Put the zucchini into another clean bowl.

6. Pour the tomato/onion mixture onto a large platter, removing and discarding the bouquet garni. Using the back of a spoon, spread it out, leaving about 1 inch around the rim of the platter. On top of the tomatoes, arrange the eggplant in a ring. Place the zucchini cubes in the middle.

7. Put the cooking juices into small pan. Bring to a boil and cook over high heat until very thick. Season to taste with salt, pepper and balsamic vinegar. Drizzle this sauce over the top of the vegetables on the platter. (If you did not have enough juice to follow this step, simply sprinkle salt, pepper, and balsamic vinegar over the top of the vegetables). Sprinkle crumbled feta cheese, then parsley, over all. Serve with wedges of pita or rice.

— Boise Urban Garden School
Boise, ID

The Gaining Ground farm occupies an historic backyard on conservation land right behind the birthplace of Henry David Thoreau in Concord, Massachusetts. Volunteers, including whole families, do much of the farming, donating the organic produce to Boston-area food pantries.

The volunteers gather in an open-air shed decorated with papier maché tomatoes for meals and informal cooking sessions. All Concord third-graders participate in a read-a-thon each spring, and most also visit the garden at least once to help on a special potato planting day.

Serve the hummus with assorted fresh vegetables and pita bread, or spread it on a whole wheat wrap and add sliced vegetables for a colorful and healthy roll-up. Look for tahini in a Middle Eastern grocery store.

ROASTED RED PEPPER HUMMUS
Makes about 2 cups

1 red bell pepper
1 (19 ounce) can chickpeas
2-3 garlic cloves
2 tablespoons sesame paste (tahini)
1/4 cup extra virgin olive oil
2 tablespoons fresh lemon juice
3/4 teaspoon salt, preferably Kosher

1. Preheat the oven to 450 degrees. Place the pepper on a baking sheet and bake for 30 minutes until soft (it will look as if it had collapsed). Wrap the pepper tightly in a sheet of aluminum foil and let it rest for 10 minutes. Open the foil. When the pepper is cool enough to handle, slip off the skin, then remove the seeds and the core. Set aside.
2. Drain the chick peas in a colander set over a sink, and rinse under running water. Peel the garlic cloves and crush them slightly (the back of a wooden spoon works well for this task).
3. In the bowl of a food processor, place the pepper, chick peas, garlic and tahini. Pulse to combine. With the motor running, add the olive oil and lemon juice. Keep the motor running until the mixture becomes a smooth puree. Season with salt.

— from the *Gaining Ground Table*
Gaining Ground
Concord, MA

Summer Salsa
Makes about 3 cups

A no-cook recipe for salsa is ideal for a hot day. Children in the summer program at the Natick Community Organic Farm near Boston made this version with the farm's heirloom tomatoes. "They loved it, as long as we didn't make it too spicy," Natasha Tauscher, their cooking instructor, reported. "One little boy was trying to chop really fast, and said, 'I'm better than the Barefoot Contessa." (The "Barefoot Contessa" is a cooking-show host and author.)

3 large (about 12 ounces each) tomatoes
4 garlic cloves
2 jalapeno peppers (or less, to taste)
1 red bell pepper
1/2 red onion
1 tablespoon olive oil
Juice of 1 lime
Chili powder, pepper and salt, to taste
Fresh scallions, cilantro or parsley, to taste

1. Chop the tomatoes. Peel and mince the garlic. Remove the seeds from the jalapeno peppers and mince the rest. Remove the seeds from the bell pepper and dice the rest into small pieces. Peel and chop the red onion into small pieces. Place all the cut vegetables into a bowl.
2. Add the remaining ingredients to the bowl and stir gently to combine. Serve with tortilla chips.

— Natick Community Organic Farm
Natick, MA

AVOCADO

If you want to know what kids like to eat, ask a student to come up with a recipe. That's what Judith Marquez, a third-grade child from New Mexico, did for this vegetable-topped snack. "I like this recipe because it is simple and easy to make. I mostly like the avocados and the crunchy tostadas," she said.

Because individual jalapeno peppers can differ in levels of heat, add just a few slices at a time to find the amount that you want. No need to overwhelm this snack with too much hot pepper!

3 ripe avocados
1 jalepeno pepper,
  or to taste
1 ripe tomato
4 ounces shredded
  cheddar cheese
12 tostada shells

1. Cut the avacados in half, remove the pits and scoop.
2. In a bowl, mash the avocado flesh with a fork. Slice the jalapeno pepper. Dice the tomato. Put the pepper and tomato in a bowl with the avocado, and mix everything together.
2. Spread the vegetable mixture over each tostada. Sprinkle the top of each one with about a tablespoon of grated cheese. The tostadas are ready to serve and eat.

Note: You can substitute canned jalapeno peppers for the fresh, adding a teaspoon or so of the canning liquid, too.

— Judith Marquez
Columbus Elementary School
Columbus, NM

98

SNACK SEED HEAVEN

The White House didn't grow sunflowers — a pity. There is no more dramatic end-of summer plant than the sunflower. These young gardeners cultivated sunflowers taller them themselves to salute the Dakota prairie.

As their sunflower seeds ripened, the Tiger Post gardeners of Ipswich, South Dakota, secured bits of old panty hose around them to keep birds away. "It looked a little funny," recalls program director Tracy Horst, "but that was the only way we could have a harvest.

But in late August and early September, eager kids decapitated sunflower plants and popped fresh seeds directly into their mouths. Those willing to wait for better flavor took them home to toast and salt with their families. Either way, Horst reports, "it was fun for the kids to notice the difference between the sunflower seeds they bought in the store and these sunflower seeds."

The crew of the Tiger Post After-School Program with its tallest crop of summer 2009.

Tiger Post Community Education Center

99

PART IV · A TIME TO REAP

Back in the White House garden, high-60s September temperatures perked up the lettuce, spinach and other leafy greens, and kept tomatoes and peppers thriving.

During this month, Michelle Obama attended the opening of a farmers' market near the grand front entrance to the White House. The FRESHFARM market takes up an entire block of Vermont Avenue to showcase the produce, meats and cheeses from nearby farms. One bakery stacks fresh loaves of bread practically up to the roof of its tent. The market is a throwback to the days when Thomas Jefferson's staff used to pull up a horse-drawn cart to buy provisions from Washington area purveyors.

"I have never seen so many people so excited about fruits and vegetables," she said to the cheers of people standing in a light drizzle. She was excited about fruits and vegetables, too. "For those of us who are battling the time crunch and those for whom access to fresh food is an issue in our neighborhoods, farmers' markets are a really important, valuable resource that we have to support."

She encouraged everyone in the neighborhood, including White House employees and workers at other nearby offices, to shop at the market. Mrs. Obama indicated that shopping at a farmers' market cuts down the space between a shopper and his or her food. She said, "That's the good thing about farmers' markets. You get to know the people who grow your food, [learn] how they do it, who they are as people. That makes a huge difference."

After she spoke, she followed her own advice and picked up some provisions that did not grow at the White House garden: eggs, cheese and chocolate milk. She also bought black kale, cherry tomatoes, mixed hot peppers, fingerling potatoes and pears, presumably to put to good use on the First Family dinner table that week.

It's true that some of what she bought was growing in her own backyard. My guess is that the vividness of the produce was particularly appealing on this gray day, and so was the ease of picking it on farm stands. Moreover, this was one way she could show her support of small, local farms.

Not that there wasn't work to be done back in her garden. A time to harvest means it's a time to dig up: carrots, and sweet potatoes. Michelle Obama spent hours digging good vegetables from the good earth. And since it was also a season for school, the Bancroft kids were back. Also helping were students from Kimball Elementary.

The time had come to dig up potatoes.

Getty Images

In October, some people delight in golden aspens and some in orange maples; others sing of harvest moons. In the District of Columbia, October is the month the Supreme Court of the United States reconvenes. On the bench in October of 2009 was Barack Obama's first Supreme Court appointment, Sonia Sotomayor. This New Yorker was likely also the first judge of Hispanic background to sit on the highest court in the land. By October, the President's children, like other Washington youngsters, had adjusted to returning to school, while adults, or those who'd enjoyed a summer holiday, were back in harness.

Reasons enough for a party. The Obamas called their October 13th celebration "Fiesta Latina", and asked New Jersey-based chef, cookbook author and Latin American cooking expert Maricel Presilla to orchestrate it. Among the guests, along with Sotomayor, were singers Gloria Estefan and Marc Anthony.

Presilla was able to raid the White House garden for fennel, which she used in arrumadinho, a Brazilian dish made with black-eyed peas. Other dishes on her menu represented other parts of Latin America, among them Argentinean beef empanadas; Honduran enchiladas with chicken hash; Guatemalan slaw and aged cheese; Cuban roast pork; and Puerto Rican pasteles.

TOMATILLOS

Tomatillos, sometimes called Mexican tomatoes, and a staple of the cuisine so loved by Michelle Obama, thrived in the White House garden. These fruits look like green cherry tomatoes with a husk that's papery on one side and sticky on the other. They can be eaten plain but taste best when roasted or simmered with other ingredients.

This recipe for Mexican-style green sauce (in Spanish, it's *salsa verde*) from Francey Hart Slater, a garden coordinator in Cambridge, Massachusetts, gives several options for cooking the tomatillos but roasting tends to yield the best flavor.

Serve the salsa with tortilla chips, quesadillas, enchiladas, grilled veggies.

SALSA VERDE
Makes about 1 cup

1/2 **pound (5-6) tomatillos**
3 **garlic cloves**
1 **onion (optional)**
Olive or canola oil, as needed for the baking sheet or the sauté pan
1/2-**inch slice of jalapeno pepper, or to taste (optional)**
Juice of 1/2 **lime**
1/4 **cup fresh cilantro leaves**
1/2 **teaspoon salt**
Freshly ground black pepper, to taste
Water, if needed

1. Husk and wash the tomatillos. The husks might be sticky, so gently tug them to remove.
2. Preheat the oven to 350 degrees. Spread a thin layer of olive or canola oil on a baking sheet. Place the whole tomatillos on the sheet, along with the garlic cloves (leave the peels on). Roast for 15-20 minutes, until they are soft and blistery. When cool enough to handle, slip the garlic cloves out of their skins.

Alternate methods of cooking the tomatillos:
Boiling: Place the whole husked tomatillos in a single layer in a pot. Add water to cover them by 1 inch. Boil until soft, about 5 minutes.
Sautéeing: Slice the tomatillos. Peel and chop the garlic cloves. In a sauté pan, heat about 1 tablespoon of olive or canola oil. Add the tomatillos and garlic (along with 1 chopped onion, optional) and cook over medium heat until soft, about 10 minutes.

To finish the salsa
Put the cooked tomatillos in a blender, along with the garlic and onion (if using). Add the jalapeno pepper (if using), lime juice, cilantro, salt and pepper. Blend until smooth. Add a little water and blend again if the sauce seems too thick.

—Francey Hart Slater
CitySprouts, Cambridge, MA

This recipe from Carolyn Blount Brodersen, a mom and a volunteer at her 6-year-old daughter's garden at the Blanche Reynolds Elementary School in Ventura, CA, promises a little razzle-dazzle in your kitchen. One minute it's a cool, green salsa for chips, another minute it's stewing with meat on the stovetop, transforming into lunch or dinner. Your choice---or do both!

1 pound fresh tomatillos
3-4 mild green or yellow chili peppers
1 cup chicken broth
1 tablespoon chopped fresh oregano
1/2 teaspoon ground cumin
2 tablespoons chopped fresh cilantro, plus additional for garnish
Salt, to taste
2 cups cooked or raw cubed meat (optional)
Sour cream, for garnish (optional)
Avocado slices, for garnish (optional)

1. Remove the husks of the tomatillos. Wash and cut each one into quarters. Slice the chili peppers in half lengthwise. Remove the seeds and dice the peppers. (Wear rubber gloves or wash your hands immediately afterwards because chili peppers can irritate your skin.)

2. Place the tomatillos and chilies in a large pot and add water to cover them. Bring to a boil over medium-high heat, then reduce the heat. Simmer for 30 minutes or until the tomatillos and chilies are tender. Drain by pouring the vegetables into a colander set in a sink. Return the vegetables to the pot.

3. Add the chicken broth, oregano and cumin. Using an immersion blender, puree the soup in the pot until it is smooth. Or puree the soup in a standard blender, working in batches if it doesn't all fit at once. If you use this type of blender, return the soup to the pot after blending.

4. Put the pot back on the stove and return the soup to a boil. Remove from the heat and stir in the cilantro. Season with salt. At this point, the mixture can be chilled and served as salsa.

5. To make mole, add 2 cups of bite-sized cubes of meat (chicken, turkey or pork---whatever you have handy) and simmer in the green salsa until heated or cooked through. (If you are using cooked meat, the time will be less.) Serve with additional fresh cilantro, sour cream, and/or avocado slices.

— Carolyn Blount Brodersen
Ventura, CA

Clara Silverstein

Chef Chriseta Comerford and two Kimball students examine bowls of tomatillos they picked.

CABBAGE

Thomas Jefferson's kitchen staff purchased cabbage 51 times from Washington markets in 1801, making it the second most popular vegetable at the White House (only lettuce was purchased more often). In 1786, Jefferson had sent seeds from Paris to Virginia for Savoy Cabbage (Chou de Milan), a cabbage with reddish veins. This type of cabbage is now part of the Jefferson Bed in the White House garden. The recipe collection from Monticello contains a recipe made of cabbage boiled with pigs' tongue –– but since I could not devise a way to make that recipe family-friendly, I'll spare you that.

With its thick leaves and strong cooking odor, I am mystified as to why "petit chou" (little cabbage) is a French endearment.

This savory recipe from the *White House Cookbook, 1894,* shouldn't be reserved only for females (despite its title). But Frances Folsom Cleveland, First Lady when the cookbook was written, must have liked it. The original description called it "very digestible and palatable." Here is an adaptation.

1 firm head green cabbage, about 2 pounds
2 eggs
1 tablespoon melted butter, plus more for greasing pan
3 tablespoons light cream
Salt and pepper, to taste

1. Cut the cabbage into quarters. Fill a large pot with water, add a little salt, and bring it to a boil. Submerge the cabbage in the water and boil for 15 minutes, or until tender, adding more boiling water as needed.
2. Drain the cabbage in a colander in the sink. Let it cool completely.
3. Preheat the oven to 350 degrees. Grease the bottom of an 8-by-8-inch baking pan with butter.
4. Core and chop the cabbage into thin pieces and place it in a mixing bowl.
5. In a separate bowl, beat the eggs. Add the melted butter (make sure it has cooled slightly, or it will cook the eggs), cream, salt and pepper. Mix well. Pour into the cabbage and mix well again.
6. Put the cabbage mixture into the baking pan and smooth out the top with the back of a spoon. Bake until the eggs are set and the casserole is heated through, 20-30 minutes.

Chef Charlie's enthusiasm and sense of humor seem to carry him far when it comes to convincing kids to try new vegetables. He started a garden at the Normal Park Elementary School in Chattanooga, Tennessee, and gives many cooking demonstrations there and at other places.

During a visit to the Isaac Dickson Elementary school in Asheville, North Carolina, he decided to do a stir-fry with every kind of cabbage he could find---white cabbage, red cabbage, Bok Choy, Napa, Savoy, all the way down in size to Brussels sprouts. One boy said "Ewwww, what's that? I'm not eating that!"

The chef was not miffed. At the lunch table, he said the boy "had his nose plugged between his fingers and had an awful look on his face." Yet he came back for more. Charlie continues, "I could tell that this was a big step for him. The next thing I knew, he and his friends were daring each other to eat the raw cabbage. They ate the entire thing! All that was left were a few gnawed-on cabbage cores."

CABBAGE STIR-FRY
Serves 4

1/2 **head of white cabbage**
1 **medium carrot**
1 **clove garlic**
1 **tablespoon tamari (Japanese-style soy sauce) or good-quality soy sauce**
1/2 **cup vegetable or chicken stock**
1 **teaspoon sugar, preferably organic cane**
1 **tablespoon sesame oil**
1 **tablespoon canola or safflower oil**
1/2 **tablespoon peeled and chopped ginger root**
1 **teaspoon chopped scallion, white part**
1/2 **teaspoon salt**

1. Cut the cabbage into thin long strips. Peel the carrot. Cut it into matchstick-size pieces or grate it on the largest part of a box grater. Peel and finely chop the garlic.
2. In a bowl, combine the tamari, stock and sugar together.
3. In a large sauté pan, heat both oils over medium-high heat. Add the ginger, scallion, garlic, and salt. Gently shake the pan for about 3 seconds and then add the vegetables (if you used grated carrots, add these about halfway through the cooking time). Quickly toss the pan a few times to cover the vegetables in oil.
4. Add the tamari-stock mixture and turn the heat to high. Let the sauce simmer until it is reduced to a glaze. Serve with brown rice and a little bit of hoisin (a type of Chinese sauce).
— Charles Loomis
Executive Chef, Greenlife Grocery
Asheville, NC and
Chattanooga, TN

HULA HOOP INTERLUDE

With a hula hoop around her waist, Michelle Obama set the tone for a Healthy Kids Fair on the White House lawn on October 21. The afternoon's guests were kids from seven Washington-area schools and their parents. Along with hula-hooping, guests could run an apolitical obstacle course set up on the lawn for the day, jump rope and literally bounce off the walls of an inflatable structure made just for this purpose, known as Moon Bounce.

Snacks made with vegetables from the White House garden were part of the event, of course. The sweet of the day was baked apples with honey from the White House hive.

WHITE HOUSE BAKED SLICED APPLES
Serves 6

This recipe is designed to be easy to make with ingredients you are likely to have already have in your kitchen. Any sturdy baking apple will do. For sweetness, try a Honey Crisp. A Granny Smith will give a more tart flavor.

6 apples
1 tablespoon butter
1/2 teaspoon ground cinnamon
1/4 cup honey, maple syrup or brown sugar
1/8 teaspoon ground nutmeg
1/2 cup rolled oats
1/2 teaspoon salt
1/4 cup raisins or any dried fruit
1/4 cup apple juice
1 cup nuts (optional)

1. Preheat the oven to 350 degrees. Wash, core, and slice the apples. Grease a baking pan with butter.
2. In a bowl, mix together the apples and the remaining ingredients. Place in the prepared pan and bake for 45 minutes, or until a golden brown crust appears.

1 medium zucchini,
    diced small
1 small onion, finely diced
1 (15 ounce) can of beans
    (white or lima)
1 tablespoon canola oil
1/2 teaspoon cumin
1/2 teaspoon chili powder
1/2 teaspoon dried parsley
    (optional)
1 1/2 cups shredded,
    reduced fat cheddar
    cheese
1/3 cup mild salsa*
6 (8 inches each) flour or
corn tortillas

Fairgoers also saw guest chefs demonstrate how schools could use free surplus foods from the Department of Agriculture to create new dishes. The recipe that follows was one of the lunch options.

1. Preheat oven to 400 degrees.
2. Wash the zucchini and peel the onion. Dice both vegetables into small pieces. Drain the beans in a colander in the sink and rinse under running water.
3. Heat the oil in a sauté pan. Add the zucchini, onion, beans, cumin and chili powder and parsley, if using. Cook until the zucchini and onion soften. Add half the cheese and continue cooking until the cheese is melted.
4. To assemble the quesadillas, place three tortillas on a non-stick baking sheet. Spread each one with some of the filling (the mixture from the pan). Top with salsa* and another tortilla. Sprinkle with the remaining cheese. Bake until the tortillas are crisp and the cheese is melted. Cut into quarters and serve warm.

* See salsa recipe page 97.

HONEY

Bees likely have been dive bombing the White House lawn since swamp flowers grew on it. The Obamas are the first White House residents to ask that a hive be put on the grounds so that they might share in the honey. The beekeeper, Charlie Brandts, is also a White House carpenter. He has a difficult job when he goes out to the hives, especially if he is using smoke to quiet the bees.

He began extracting honey from the hive in June and removed the last of it in November. The taste of the honey changed according to what kinds of flowers the bees were visiting. They had their pick of cherry, clover and basswood blossoms at the nearby Washington Monument;the bees enjoyed licorice-y anise hyssop at home. Honey made its way into many White House meals.

The bees' house is a sort of split-level contemporary unlike the classical home First Families occupy. The hive is boxy, with each box containing sliding frames –– they go up and down for easy removal –– a fact probably lost on the bees when they move in. During the course of their residence, the bees keep naturally busy filling frame cells with the fruit of their labor: honey. The bees signal a full frame by capping their work with beeswax. Then along comes Brandts who whooshes the frame away.

Like many people with good connections to beekeepers, Mrs. Obama gave away jars of honey as gifts. In her case, the packaging was really special. Having decided to give take-home remembrances to the spouses of visiting world leaders at the G-20 Pittsburgh Summit, she used hand-blown glass vases designed exclusively for the occasion, and signed the tag on each one.

All told, the White House hive produced 134 pounds of honey in its first season — about 11 gallons.

It accompanied baked apples and livened up salad dressings. It also sweetened White House cupcakes and Halloween treats.

Clara Silverstein

The bee hive at 1600 Pennsylvania Avenue

WHITE HOUSE HONEY CUPCAKES
Makes 12 cupcakes

Cupcakes:
1/4 **cup butter, left out on the counter for approximately 1 hour to soften**
1/4 **cup sugar**
3/4 **cup honey**
2 **eggs**
1/2 **cup buttermilk**
1/2 **teaspoon vanilla**
2 **cups flour**
1 **tablespoon baking powder**
1/4 **teaspoon salt**

Icing:
2 **cups powdered sugar**
1/2 **cup honey**
3 **tablespoons lemon juice**

For the cupcakes:
1. Preheat the oven to 350 degrees. Line a 12-cup muffin tin with paper liners.
2. In the bowl of an electric stand mixer on high speed, cream the butter and sugar until light and fluffy. On medium speed, mix in the honey, eggs, buttermilk and vanilla until blended.
3. In a separate bowl, sift together the flour, baking powder and salt. On medium speed, mix into the batter until just blended. Scoop the batter evenly into the lined muffin cups.
4. Bake about 20 minutes; cupcakes are done when the tops spring back lightly to the touch or a toothpick inserted in the center comes out clean.

For the icing:
1. Place the icing ingredients in a small saucepan. Over medium heat, whisk the ingredients until the sugar and honey dissolve together; keep whisking to avoid clumps.
2. Using a spoon, drizzle over the tops of the cupcakes, or carefully pour over the cupcakes.

— Obama Foodorama Blog

Yosses uses honey from the White House beehive in the cupcake batter as well as the icing. He does not specify how to decorate the cupcakes, but if you want to keep with the garden theme, place a sprig of fresh herbs on top of each one.

(ALMOST) LAST HARVEST

On an overcast November afternoon, Mrs. Obama, dressed in a sweater and sneakers, pulled on a pair of garden gloves and set to work with children from the Bancroft and Kimball elementary schools. White House cooks joined in. All hands were needed to pick the best of the last for the Kitchen Garden Harvest Festival.

Michelle Obama pried out a sweet potato and lifted it from the earth. It was far bigger than what you usually see at a supermarket — almost the size of a small football. She held it up and said, "Now this is a sweet potato! Let's see who can get the biggest."

The children laughed, then went back to unearthing potatoes, some with their bare hands. They placed the potatoes, still caked with dirt, on the ground, and later loaded them into a wheelbarrow. One boy pointed to an especially large sweet potato and said, "Whoever likes that must have a biiiiig mouth!"

Other children teamed up with chefs to pick green peppers and put them into large metal bowls. The weather was cool enough for sweatshirts but as the children worked, they pulled them off and tied them around their waists or dropped them at picnic tables covered with red and white checkered cloths.

The garden was swarming with kids squatting, lifting, pulling, and shaking plants. Occasionally, a bee from the hive buzzed through.

Kass called out, "Who wants to help with the turnips? All of these have to come out, too." A group of students soon appeared.

At one edge of the garden, kids weighed vegetables then helped sort them into boxes and plastic bins for donation to Miriam's

Kitchen. They asked questions. They giggled over the shapes of eggplant, broccoli and kohlrabi.

Most of them did not seem to be nibbling, but someone in the group with the kohlrabi announced authoritatively, "You can eat the leaves." Apparently, one boy already had. "I need a flavor---my mouth is so fresh!" he said.

One of the last vegetables to be weighed in was fennel with ferns on top of the bulb, bobbing in all directions. The ferns tickled the face of whoever was carrying it, including Mrs. Obama. When her arms were empty, several kids clustered around her and she hugged them and smilingly posed for photos.

Earlier she had told them that over 740 pounds of food had already come out of "this little piece of land."

Kass asked, "Who is going to eat all their vegetables tonight?" and was answered by a chorus of "Me!"

THE COOKS CAME OUT TO PLAY

Assistant chef David Luerson (far right) joins the kids picking peppers. In the foreground, the broccoli is going strong.

A CORNUCOPIA OF FALL TREASURES

Top row: Red romaine and sweet potatoes
Bottom row: peppers and arugula

Clara Silverstein all three photos

FENNEL

Fennel, a favorite in Italy, has a giant, pale green bulb and a stalk that looks like celery with fronds on top. The stalk can be eaten but the bulb is generally considered the best part. It crunches like an apple but tastes a bit like licorice. It can be grated into a salad, boiled, or sliced and grilled. Italians like to dip raw slices in olive oil, then dip them in salt.

FENNEL-PARSNIP PUREE
Serves 4

1/2 **pound parsnips (3-4)**
1/2 **pound fennel (1 bulb, stems and leafy parts removed)**
2 **tablespoons unsalted butter**
1-2 **tablespoons chopped fresh dill or parsley**
Salt and pepper, to taste

1. Peel the parsnips and cut off the ends. Cut into ½-inch chunks. Place in 2-quart saucepan.
2. Cut the fennel bulb in half and then cut out the white, triangular core at the bottom. Cut the fennel into ½-inch pieces. Place in the saucepan.
3. Add enough water to the saucepan to cover the vegetables. They should just begin to float. Sprinkle with about 1 teaspoon of salt. Bring the water to a boil over medium-high heat. Reduce the heat to a simmer. Cook for about 20 minutes, until it's easy to poke the vegetables with a fork.
4. Drain the water using a colander set over a sink.
5. Let cool slightly and place the vegetables in a food processor. Add the butter and turn on the motor. Keep processing the vegetables until they are fairly smooth.
6. Place the vegetables in a bowl. Stir in the dill or parsley, salt and pepper.

— Melissa Graham
Purple Asparagus
Chicago, IL

1 bulb fennel
1 pear
Juice from 1/2 lemon
Salt, to taste
1-2 tablespoons chopped fennel fronds, optional

1. Wash the fennel, cutting off and saving the fronds. Slice the bulb into very thin strips.
2. Wash and core the pear, and slice it into equally thin strips.
3. Put the fennel and pear in a bowl. Squeeze the lemon juice over the top and sprinkle with salt. Add the fennel fronds and toss gently to combine everything. Cover and refrigerate until ready to serve.

— Joanna Sooper
Milwaukie, OR

In this simple salad, the pears and fennel bring out the best in each other. Make the recipe a few hours before you want to serve it so the lemon juice can draw out the flavors. You can add fresh herbs, such as mint or parsley or a chopped scallion.

This recipe was devised by an Oregon teacher then sent to us by an enthusiastic parent.

Feathery fennel was a late autumn bonus along with sweet potatoes and Kohlrabi .

Clara Silverstein

KOHLRABI

This vegetable, a bulb topped with leaves that poke up and sprout in all directions, would hardly win any beauty contests. Nor is its sharp flavor — a cross between cabbage and turnip, which is actually what the word kohlrabi means in German — usually a favorite with kids. Yet kohlrabi delivers a healthy dose of Vitamin C. Do try it.

Leave it to Charlie Loomis, the chef who managed to make cabbage appealing to a group of North Carolina schoolchildren, to come up with a tasty recipe for kohlrabi. The spices and tomatoes in this dish tone down the vegetable's harsh flavor.

1 pound kohlrabi (2-3 heads)
2 large carrots
2 cloves garlic
2 tablespoons of extra-virgin olive oil
1 teaspoon dried thyme
1/2 teaspoon cumin seeds
4 medium sized tomatoes (see note) or 1 (15-ounce) can diced tomatoes
1/4 teaspoon turmeric
1 1/2 teaspoons salt, or to taste
Freshly ground black pepper, to taste
1 cup chicken, beef or vegetable stock

1. Cut about 1 inch off the bottom of the kohlrabi. Trim off the stems and leaves. Peel the rest of the skin off with a potato peeler and discard. Cut the kohlrabi into 1-inch pieces as you would a potato. Peel the carrots and cut into 1-inch pieces. Peel and chop the garlic.
2. In a medium saucepan over medium-high heat, heat the olive oil. After about 1 minute, add the kohlrabi, carrots, thyme, cumin seeds and garlic. Sauté for about 1 minute.
3. Peel the tomatoes (see below for directions), dice them, and add them to the pot. If using canned tomatoes, add them to the pot along with their liquid. Add the turmeric, salt and pepper. Add the stock and bring the mixture to a simmer (not a boil).
4. Turn the heat to low and cover the pot loosely with a lid. Simmer until the carrots and kohlrabi are tender, about 1 hour. Season with more salt and pepper if needed. Serve plain or with rice.

To peel tomatoes:
With the tip of a sharp knife, cut an X on the bottom of the tomato. Place a bowl of ice water near the stove. Bring a pot of water to a boil. Gently drop in the tomato and let it boil for about 1 minute. Immediately remove the tomato (a slotted spoon works well for this), then plunge it into the ice water. The skin should peel right off. The same technique works for peaches, too.

— Charles Loomis, Greenlife Grocery
Asheville, NC, and Chattanooga, TN

116

TURNIPS

The Romans were fond of turnips, but we usually don't think of this earthy-tasting vegetable as a banquet delicacy. Nowadays, turnips are mostly known for two things: roots that contribute to good soups, and greens that can be cooked like other leafy vegetables.

The combination of turnips and greens in this recipe from Oakland Based Urban Gardens (OBUGS) makes this an ideal cool-weather recipe — not that the East Bay has the large temperature changes of Washington, D.C. The long growing season means that OBUGS can run its gardens for most of the year. Clearly, one third-grader has benefited. "What I like most is when you grow the vegetables, you pull them out, and you cook them. The number one vegetable, my favorite, is the onion. No matter where I live, I'll plant seeds," the student wrote.

1 onion
5 cloves garlic
4 bunches (approximately 3 pounds total) collard greens
1 bunch (approximately 1 pound) mustard greens
2 turnips
2 tablespoons vegetable oil, such as canola
Salt and pepper, to taste
Rice vinegar, to taste, optional

1. Peel and finely chop the onion and garlic.
2. Wash the collards and mustard greens well. Remove the stems and cut the leaves into thin strips.
3. Wash and peel the turnips and chop them into small chunks.
4. In a large pot, heat the oil over medium-high heat. Add the onion and garlic. Sauté for 2 minutes. Add the turnips and stir to mix them with the other ingredients.
5. Add the greens and a dash of water (about ¼ cup). Stir for 2 minutes. Cook for 10-15 minutes, stirring occasionally and adding more water if the mixture becomes dry, or until the greens become tender. Add the salt, pepper and rice vinegar, if using, just before serving.

—Oakland Based Urban Gardens (OBUGS)
Oakland. CA

117

RADISH

Radishes come in many varieties, in colors ranging from the familiar pinkish-red to black. The ancient pharaohs liked to eat radishes, and so did the Greeks. This root vegetable belongs to the mustard family, which may explain its slightly sharp flavor. The White House grew many types of radishes, including the exotic white icicles, which look like white carrots and are supposed to be milder than other types.

Serve this salad in a white bowl to show off the contrasting red and green. This New Hampshire group, who created this recipe, has many other great ideas for using radishes: toss them into stir fries, sprinkle them on tuna or egg salad, and place them on bagels spread with cream cheese.

To pep up a regional favorite, these young gardeners have even been known to place a few sliced radishes on top of New England clam chowder (this cream-based chowder is always white — tomato-based chowder is Manhattan style).

2 pounds green beans
6-8 radishes
2 cloves garlic
1/2 cup olive oil
1 tablespoon apple cider vinegar
Zest and juice of 1 lemon
Salt and pepper, to taste
2 tablespoons thinly sliced fresh
parsley leaves

1. Halfway fill a large pot with water, sprinkle in some salt, and bring it to a boil. Place a bowl of ice water near the sink.
2. Wash the beans and remove the spiky stem ends. Place the beans in the boiling water to blanch for 2-3 minutes, or until the color brightens.
3. Drain the beans in a colander in the sink, then immediately place them in the ice water to stop them from cooking. When they are cool, drain again.
4. Wash the radishes and cut them horizontally into circular slices.
5. Peel and chop the garlic.
6. In a large bowl, whisk together the garlic, olive oil, vinegar, lemon juice and zest.
7. Add the beans and radishes to the bowl and toss to coat with dressing.
8. Add the salt, pepper and parsley, and toss again.

— Kids Can Grow
University of New Hampshire Cooperative Extension
Dover, NH

This salad's assortment of fall vegetables echoes the colors of the leaves. Edible nasturtium blossoms, if you can find them, add a splash of orange. Any kind of radish will do, so the White House's exotic varieties would fit right in. Tania and Susanne, instructors at the New York Botanical Garden's Ruth Rea Howell Family Garden, were equally adept at planting, picking, and chopping vegetables with kids.

Salad:
10 lettuce leaves (from approximately 1 head lettuce)
1 bunch (6-8 leaves) tender chard
1 bunch bok choy or baby bok choy (6-8 leaves)
4 carrots
1 bunch (6-8) radishes, all types
10-12 nasturtium blossoms, or to taste, optional

Dressing:
2 tablespoons fresh lemon juice
1 tablespoon white wine vinegar or cider vinegar
6 tablespoons extra-virgin olive oil
1 teaspoon prepared mustard, or to taste
Salt and pepper, to taste
1 teaspoon honey, or to taste

For the salad:
1. Wash the lettuce, chard, and bok choy. Remove the tough stems from the chard. Cut all three types of greens into thin, ribbon-shaped slices. Place them in a bowl.
2. Peel and grate or dice the carrots. Wash and dice the radishes. Place them in the bowl.
3. Place the nasturtium blossoms on top. Serve with honey-mustard dressing.

For the dressing:
1. In a bowl, whisk together the lemon juice, vinegar and olive oil.
2. Add the mustard, salt and pepper, and whisk to combine.
3. Add the honey, whisking again before serving.

— Ruth Rea Howell Family Garden,
New York Botanical Garden
Bronx, NY

Nasturtium

119

CARROTS

Carrots were originally yellow or purple. Dutch farmers bred the orange variety in the 17th century to honor their royal House of Orange, giving us the color that we still associate with carrots. Carrots, interestingly, are related to Queen Anne's Lace, white and pretty but a roadside weed, nonetheless.

With Elmo and three children at her side on the set of "Sesame Street," Michelle Obama planted vegetables in a tabletop bed filled with dirt. One girl sprinkled in tomato seeds, followed by a boy with cucumbers and a girl with lettuce. When it was Mrs. Obama's turn, she and Elmo planted carrots. "Look at how tiny those seeds are!" Elmo exclaimed.

"They are, but these little seeds are going to make for some great-tasting food," answered Mrs. Obama.

Gawky Big Bird came out to interrupt them, asking the First Lady if she ate the seeds. He said he loved to eat seeds, and asked if she was part bird. She laughed and said, "No, I'm not." She set him straight. "You see, I really don't eat these kinds of seeds at all. But I do eat what grows from these seeds." She held up a basket, and the vegetable-puppets inside piped up and said, "Let's hear it for the First Lady." Everyone cheered.

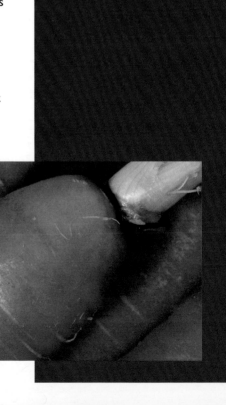

Most kids would turn their noses up at a lumpy looking soup like this, but when they help cook, it's a totally different story. The recipe starts out a bit like stone soup. To boiling water, children add carrots, celery and spinach from the school garden. When it's all done, they say it's the most amazing soup they've ever had, reports Kelly Atterton, parent of a kindergartener at the Wonderland Avenue School in Los Angeles. The red lentils give the soup a beautiful orange glow, but if you can't find red lentils, brown ones will do.

If the finished soup tastes too plain, perk up the flavor with more salt, pepper, hot sauce or chopped fresh parsley.

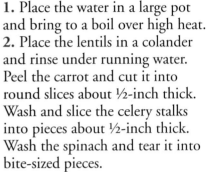

6 cups water
1 cup red lentils
6 carrots
3 stalks celery
3/4 cup spinach
1/2 teaspoon cumin
1/2 teaspoon turmeric
1/2 teaspoon ground coriander
1/2 cup uncooked, medium-sized pasta, such as elbows or shells
2 tablespoons butter
Salt to taste

1. Place the water in a large pot and bring to a boil over high heat.
2. Place the lentils in a colander and rinse under running water. Peel the carrot and cut it into round slices about ½-inch thick. Wash and slice the celery stalks into pieces about ½-inch thick. Wash the spinach and tear it into bite-sized pieces.
3. When the water boils, add the lentils to the pot. Toss in the cumin, turmeric, and coriander. Add the carrots, celery and spinach. Lower the heat on the stove, cover the pot, and let the soup simmer for 35 minutes.
4. Add the pasta. Simmer the soup for another 10 minutes. Add the butter and salt, and stir.

— Wonderland Ave. School
Los Angeles, CA

Baby Carrots with Orange Juice and Cinnamon
Serves 4

1/2 **pound baby carrots or full size carrots, cut into quarters**
1 tablespoon butter
1 teaspoon cinnamon
2 tablespoons to 1/4 **cup orange juice**
Carrot greens for garnish (optional)

1. Wash and clean the carrots.
2. In a saucepan, melt the butter over medium heat. Add the carrots. Sauté, stirring occasionally, until the carrots start to brown on the edges.
3. Add the cinnamon and mix to coat the carrots.
4. Drizzle 2 tablespoons of the orange juice over the carrots and stir. If you like more sauce, add the entire ¼ cup of juice at once. Cook until the orange juice becomes bubbly and starts to evaporate, then garnish and serve.

— School Garden
Project of Lane County
Eugene, OR

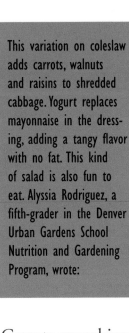

This variation on coleslaw adds carrots, walnuts and raisins to shredded cabbage. Yogurt replaces mayonnaise in the dressing, adding a tangy flavor with no fat. This kind of salad is also fun to eat. Alyssia Rodriguez, a fifth-grader in the Denver Urban Gardens School Nutrition and Gardening Program, wrote:

Carrots crunching
in my mouth

They have that
sweet sound

Like the sound of
leaves crunching

As you walk on
them

Underneath the
trees

Salad:
1/4 **cup shredded cabbage**
1/4 **cup finely diced carrots**
1 **tablespoon finely diced
red pepper**
1 **tablespoon chopped walnuts**
1 **tablespoon raisins**

Dressing:
2 **tablespoons non-fat plain
or vanilla yogurt**
1/2 **teaspoon canola oil**
1 **teaspoon cider vinegar**
1 **teaspoon sugar or honey**
Dash of celery seed

For the salad:
In a bowl, mix the salad ingredients.

For the dressing:
1. Place the dressing ingredients in a jar with a tight-fitting lid. Shake and pour over the salad.
2. Mix lightly and serve.

— Denver Urban Gardens
Denver, CO

THANKSGIVING

Many history books tell us that the Pilgrims and the Indians held an autumn harvest feast in 1621 when the New World was barely settled. Some Virginians counter that the first Thanksgiving service was held at Berkeley on the James River on December 4, 1619.

In 1789, George Washington petitioned to make November 26 a national day of "public thanksgiving." But it wasn't until the 1840s, when James K. Polk was in office, that the first Thanksgiving dinner was held at the White House. Abraham Lincoln issued a Thanksgiving Proclamation in 1863. The fourth Thursday in November finally became a legal holiday in 1941. In 1947, Harry S. Truman started the annual White House tradition of pardoning a turkey before Thanksgiving. Different china patterns have come and gone, but turkey, cranberries, and pumpkin seem to be on the table to stay.

On the day before their first White House Thanksgiving, the President and his family, including Michelle's mother, Marian Robinson, handed grocery items to the needy at Martha's Pantry in Washington, D.C. The Obamas believe it's important for them to find time each year to personally serve the less fortunate.

The next day's White House Thanksgiving dinner was for 50; the family invited some friends and staff. The traditional menu included turkey with cornbread stuffing or oyster stuffing, greens, macaroni and cheese, sweet potatoes, mashed potatoes and a green bean casserole. There were six flavors of pie: Banana cream, pumpkin, apple, sweet potato, huckleberry and cherry.

Getty Images

The entire Obama family were volunteers on the day before Thanksgiving

SWEET POTATOES

Don't confuse sweet potatoes with yams –– they are similar, but sweet potatoes are native to the Americas, while starchy yams come from Africa.

Michelle Obama has said that the First Family is particularly fond of sweet potatoes. This recipe gets its flavor from a subtle mix of spices, plus citrus juices and just a bit of butter (or margarine). The sweet potatoes add just the right amount of sweetness, but with no added sugar, this certainly qualifies as a healthy addition to the table at Thanksgiving or any other holiday.

WHITE HOUSE WHIPPED SWEET POTATOES
Serves 4

3 medium (12 to 16 ounces each) sweet potatoes
2 tablespoons butter
1/8 **teaspoon ground cinnamon**
1/8 **teaspoon ground cumin**
1/8 **teaspoon chili powder**
Pinch of ground cloves
4 tablespoons orange juice
1 tablespoon freshly squeezed lemon juice
Salt to taste

1. Set the oven at 425 degrees.
2. Wash the potatoes, pat dry, and wrap each one in foil. Place on a baking sheet and bake until soft all the way through, approximately one hour (cooking time will vary depending on the size of the potatoes).
3. Remove the potatoes from the oven. Unwrap the foil and allow them to cool enough to handle.
4. Cut each potato in half. Scoop out the inside and place in a large mixing bowl.
5. Add the butter, cinnamon, cumin, chili powder, cloves, orange juice, and lemon juice. Using an electric mixer with a whisk attachment on medium speed, whip the potatoes until smooth and all the ingredients are incorporated, 1 to 2 minutes.
6. Add the salt and serve.

Serves 8

Crust:
10 ounces unsalted butter, kept cold
3 ounces lard, kept cold (or substitute solid vegetable shortening)
3 cups flour
1/4 cup sugar
1 1/2 teaspoons salt
1/2 cup ice water

Filling:
2 pounds apples
1 cup sugar
1/2 cup honey
1/3 cup cornstarch
1 teaspoon vanilla extract
1/4 teaspoon cinnamon
Zest and juice of 1 lemon

Egg wash:
1 egg
1 teaspoon salt
Sugar, for sprinkling

For the crust:
1. Cut the butter and lard or vegetable shortening into small chunks. In a food processor, pulse together the flour, sugar and salt. Add the butter and lard, then pulse briefly until the mixture forms small crumbs. Add the ice water and pulse just until a dough forms.
2. Divide the dough into 2 pieces and shape into disks. Wrap each disk in plastic wrap and refrigerate at least 1 hour or overnight.
3. When chilled, prepare the pie shell: On a floured surface, use a rolling pin to roll out one disk to a 14-inch circle. Transfer the dough to a deep 9-inch pie pan, leaving a 1-inch overhang. Refrigerate the crust in the pan for at least 30 minutes or overnight.
4. When ready to bake the bottom crust, heat the oven to 375 degrees. Line the cold crust with foil and fill with baking weights, rice or dry beans to hold it in place. Bake the pie shell for 30 minutes and remove from oven. Leave the oven on once the crust is done. While the crust is baking, prepare the filling.

APPLE PIE

For the filling:
1. Peel and core the apples; cut them into chunks. In a large saucepan, toss together the apples, sugar, honey, cornstarch, vanilla, cinnamon, lemon zest and juice. Let sit for 20 minutes.
2. Bring the fruit mixture to a boil over medium heat. Cook, stirring occasionally to prevent sticking until the fruit thickens. Let cool.
3. When the filling has cooled, pour it into the baked crust.

For the top crust and egg wash:
1. Roll out the second disk of dough to a 12-inch circle.
2. In a small bowl, beat the egg with the salt. Use a pastry brush to brush the egg on the edges of the cooked crust. Place the top crust over the filling. Using a fork or crimper, gently crimp the top crust, sealing the pie around the edges.
3. With a paring knife, slit the top of the crust in several places to create steam vents. Brush the egg wash over the crust, then sprinkle with the sugar.
4. Bake for another 30 to 40 minutes, or until the filling is bubbling and the top crust is golden brown. Let cool for 1 to 2 hours before serving.

— Obama Foodorama Blog

PART V

THE GARDEN IN WINTER

In mid-December, the White House tallied the weight of the fruits and vegetables harvested during its inaugural season. Sam Kass reported it at 1,007 pounds, over half a ton and more than planners had predicted.

The $180 cost of fertilizer and seeds was not excessive for so large a garden with such outstanding first-year output. Seeds amounted to $55 of that expense.

The coming of winter brought innovation and additional cost. Much of the garden was replanted in rye to rebalance the soil and prevent erosion. The chief innovation was the installation of hoop houses to extend the growing season and give a jumpstart to some 2010 plantings. A hoop house is a plastic or cloth covered frame that looks like a cross between a tent and a caterpillar, such as you may have seen in commercial garden centers.

The cover absorbs and traps sun-generated heat, keeping the plants from freezing at night in moderate climates. Under the hoops, White House gardeners planted hardy crops: Spinach, lettuce, carrots, mustard greens, chard and cabbage.

Good thing the hoop houses were finished before a record-setting two feet of snow fell on the nation's capital on December 18 and 19. Some plants even survived the sustained freezing temperatures of the new year.

WHITE HOUSE GARDEN HOOP HOUSES

Eddie Gehman Kohan/ObamaFoodorama.com

HOLIDAY COLORS

"I especially look forward to cooking with the spinach," Kass had said before the winter holidays. "Winter spinach is extra sweet. Sugar doesn't freeze, so spinach produces extra sugars in the winter to protect itself from frost. It tastes almost like candy."

POMEGRANATE

This recipe is named Christmas Salad because of its green and red colors. Liz Van Brunt makes this salad with her own children, Alex, 15, and Jacob, 12. They have fun taking apart the pomegranate and oranges. (Wear an apron or old clothes because pomegranate juice can stain.) The honey-sweetened dressing is also a hit. Best of all, in the boys' view, it tastes nothing like the cooked spinach they don't like.

Salad:
4-6 cups baby spinach
2 tablespoons fresh basil leaves
1/2 **cup sliced almonds**
1/2 **fresh pomegranate, or** 1/4 **cup dried cranberries or dried cherries (See Note)**
1 large navel orange or 4 clementines

Dressing:
1/2 **tablespoon olive oil**
1 tablespoon honey
2 1/2 **teaspoons vinegar**
1/2 **teaspoon poppy seeds**
1/4 **cup orange juice**

Note: Pomegranates are available in supermarkets from September through December.

For the salad:
1. Wash and dry the spinach and the basil. Chop or use scissors to cut the basil into small pieces. Place the spinach and basil in a large bowl.
2. Line the tray of a toaster oven with foil. Place the almonds in a single layer on the tray. Toast until slightly brown, about 2-3 minutes. Watch carefully so they do not burn! Remove them from the oven and let them cool.
3. Cut the pomegranate in half. Over the sink or a large bowl, use a spoon or your fingers to gently pry out the seeds. Your hands will get red and sticky! Put the seeds in the salad bowl.
4. Peel the orange and separate the slices. Cut each segment in half. Put them in the bowl.
5. Toss all the salad ingredients together except the almonds.

For the dressing:
Mix the dressing ingredients in a small bowl until blended. Pour on the salad just before serving. Top with almonds.

— Liz Van Brunt
Children's Cooking Instructor
Chautauqua, NY and Frederick, MD

131

MORE HOLIDAY TREATS

The lighting of the National Christmas Tree outside the fence at the White House on December 4 gave a bright and energy-efficient start to the holiday season, thanks to LED instead of incandescent bulbs. The indoor Christmas tree was especially lovely, hung with ornaments decorated by 60 community groups around the nation.

Meanwhile in the kitchen, Bill Yosses and his staff were melting and molding 250 pounds of white chocolate for their gingerbread replica of the White House. The 150 pounds of gingerbread dough contained White House honey. Upholding this holiday tradition required ingenuity as well as a saw to cut some of the thickest slabs of gingerbread.

To keep every detail of the building current, the pastry staff made sure to add a marzipan replica of the First Dog, Bo (who had his own Christmas stocking), as well as the garden. There were exquisite miniature baskets of carrots, eggplants, and cabbage as well as the hand-lettered signs labeling each one. Everything on the house was edible, except a light fixture inside a shadowbox view of the State Dining Room.

"We have such a great time planning, baking and decorating, but each year the best part is always seeing the reactions of visitors from across the country when they first see our gingerbread house on their tour of the actual White House," said Yosses, who also baked for George W. and Laura Bush.

This replica inspired another faux White House across town at the U.S. Botanical Garden. Most of this house was made of natural materials (as in bark and leaves), and it included a greenery-constructed garden, complete with stone pathways between the garden beds.

The holidays at the real White House brought in thousands of visitors for tours and receptions, keeping the kitchen staff working hard, but also giving the Obamas a chance to enjoy seasonal treats more than once. When Oprah Winfrey came to interview the Obamas, the President joked, "Santa can eat what he wants," presumably including many, many plates of cookies. So can Barack Obama, to judge from the lean look of him.

The holidays were not a time of taboo foods for the First Family. Michelle Obama has declared: "If I'm eating the right things — and I tell my girls this — if you're getting the right foods for most of the time, then when it's time to have cake and French fries on those special occasions, then you balance it out."

Anyone who has worked as hard on planning and promoting a garden as Michelle Obama has deserves a treat. To her we recommend Martha Washington's Great Cake, served at George and Martha's Mount Vernon, Virginia, home at Christmas and other special occasions.

And, dear reader, you and your family, especially if it's large, might want to try that cake, too. It's also possible that you'd like the Spice Bar Christmas Cookies served as a holiday sweet at the Clinton White House in 1996 or Michelle Obama's holiday shortbread.

I'm pretty sure that if Michelle was sitting beside you right now, she'd say: It's the holiday season: take your pick.

Created by Applied Imagination, photo by Paul Busse

Makes approximately 60 cookies (2-inches long by 1-inch wide)

Cookies:
1/2 **cup (1 stick) unsalted butter, at room temperature**
1 **cup sugar**
2 **large eggs**
1/2 **cup molasses**
1 **teaspoon cinnamon**
1/2 **teaspoon mace or nutmeg**
Pinch of salt
1 **teaspoon lemon zest**
1 1/2 **teaspoons baking soda dissolved in 3 tablespoons water**
3 **cups flour**
1/2 **cup sliced toasted almonds**
1/4 **cup diced candied orange peel**
1/4 **cup diced candied lemon peel**
1 **cup semisweet chocolate chips or white chocolate chips**
Colored sugar or sprinkles

1. In a bowl, using an electric mixer, beat the butter and sugar until creamy. Beat in the eggs one at a time.

2. Add the molasses, cinnamon, mace or nutmeg, salt and lemon zest, and beat to combine.

3. In a small bowl, dissolve the baking soda in the water. Add to the butter mixture and beat to combine.

4. Beat in the flour 1 cup at a time.

5. With a spoon, stir in the almonds, orange and lemon peel.

6. Wrap the dough in plastic wrap and refrigerate for at least 1 hour or as long as overnight.

7. When ready to bake, preheat the oven to 350 degrees. Line two baking sheets with parchment paper.

8. Divide the dough into 3 equal portions. Place one portion on a baking sheet. Using your hands (rub a little flour on them to keep the dough from sticking) or a spatula, shape the dough into a log approximately 10 inches long by 3 inches wide by ¼-inch thick. Repeat with the other portions. You can fit two portions on one baking sheet as long as you keep them 4 inches apart.

9. Bake until firm, 14 -15 minutes. Cool before cutting into 1-by-2 inch bars.

10. When the cookies are completely cool, melt the chocolate. Brush a little over the top of each cookie and sprinkle with colored sugar or sprinkles.

To: Bill and Hillary

These chewy cookies, adapted from a 20th-century recipe, strike a good balance between spices, nuts, and candied citrus fruits. The topping of melted chocolate does the double duty of enhancing the flavor and keeping the decorative sugar from sliding off. Trays of these made the holiday party rounds at the White House when Bill and Hillary Clinton lived there.

While our fledgling nation's capital was in New York, President Washington went home to Mount Vernon for Christmas. George and Martha had to be prepared for dozens of holiday callers, many of them unbidden. The recipe from the nation's original First Lady called for 40 eggs and four pounds of butter. Still, the original cake was only a single large layer.

This cake traditionally was served for Twelfth Night (January 6), also known as Epiphany, which is the last of the 12 days of Christmas. The 18th-century recipe for frosting suggested brushing it on the cake with a bundle of feathers! No need for that in this version, adapted by the Mount Vernon Ladies' Association, which maintains the Washington home.

If you can't find orange flower water at a specialty food shop or Middle Eastern grocery, substitute orange liqueur, such as Cointreau or Triple Sec.

Serves 12-16

Cake:
10 eggs
1 pound (2 cups) butter
1 pound (2 cups) sugar
11/4 pounds (20 ounces) flour
1 1/4 pounds (20 ounces) fruit (see note)
2 1/2 teaspoons ground mace
2 1/2 teaspoons ground nutmeg
2 ounces (1/4 cup) wine, such as Madeira or cream sherry
2 ounces (1/4 cup) French brandy

Note: Mrs. Washington would have used any fresh fruit that was seasonal or available dried, including nuts, which were considered a fruit. You can choose whatever you like. One combination that works successfully: 1 large pear, cored and diced; 2 medium to large apples, peeled cored and diced; 3 ½ ounces of raisins; and 2 ounces (about ½ cup) sliced almonds.

1. Preheat the oven to 350 degrees. Lightly grease a 10-inch springform cake pan. Sprinkle in some flour, tap the bottom of the pan and rotate it to coat the bottom and sides with flour. Discard any excess flour that does not stick to the pan.
2. Separate the egg whites from the yolks into two separate bowls and set the yolks aside. Using an electric mixer, beat the egg whites to the "soft peak" stage. (They will make small mounds when you lift the beater, but the tops will flop over; they should not be stiff.)
3. In another bowl, beat the butter until it is creamy.
4. Slowly add the beaten egg whites, one spoonful at a time, to the butter, beating to incorporate.
5. Add the sugar slowly to egg whites and butter; again, one spoonful at a time, beating to incorporate.

6. Add the egg yolks, beating to incorporate.

7. Add flour, slowly, beating to incorporate.

8. Stir in the fruit.

9. Stir in the ground mace, nutmeg, wine, and brandy.

10. Put the batter into the pan and place it in the oven. Bake for about 75 minutes, until the center is firm.

11. Remove the cake from the oven and cool completely before frosting it.

Frosting:
3 egg whites
1 1/2 cups confectioner's sugar
1 teaspoon grated lemon peel
2 tablespoons orange flower water (available at specialty or Middle Eastern food shops)

1. Preheat the oven to 200 degrees.

2. In a bowl using an electric mixer, beat the egg whites with 2 tablespoons of the sugar for 3 minutes. Continue adding the sugar, 2 tablespoons at a time, until you have added it all.

3. Add the lemon peel and orange flower water. Continue beating until the icing is stiff enough to stay parted when you cut through it with a knife.

4. Smooth the icing onto the top and sides of the cake. Place it in the oven and let it dry and harden for 1 hour. This icing will be brittle and shatters when you cut into the cake. Don't be surprised when that happens.

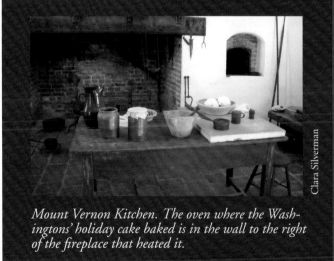

Mount Vernon Kitchen. The oven where the Washingtons' holiday cake baked is in the wall to the right of the fireplace that heated it.

— Courtesy of the Mount Vernon Ladies' Association

MICHELLE OBAMA'S HOLIDAY SHORTBREAD COOKIES
Makes about 6 dozen

This recipe became widely circulated in 2008 as part of a contest sponsored by *Family Circle*. During each presidential campaign since 1992, the magazine has run a cookie contest between the spouses of the candidates. Mrs. Obama's shortbread cookies went up against Cindy McCain's oatmeal-butterscotch cookies and Bill Clinton's oatmeal cookies (at the time, Hillary Clinton was still a candidate). Readers could vote for their favorites. Though the McCain cookies won, the citrus-accented Obama cookies hold their own.

1 1/2 **cups unsalted butter, left out on the counter for about 1 hour to soften**
1 1/2 **cups plus**
   2 tablespoons sugar
2 **egg yolks**
3 **cups cake flour**
   (not self-rising)
1 **teaspoon each orange and lemon zest**
2 **tablespoons Amaretto (almond liqueur)**
1/4 **teaspoon salt**
1 **beaten egg white**
Chopped nuts or dried fruit, optional

1. Preheat the oven to 325 degrees.
2. In a bowl, using an electric mixer, mix together the butter and 1½ cups of sugar.
3. Add the egg yolks, one at a time, and beat until smooth.
4. Stir in flour, zest, amaretto and salt, and mix only until everything is incorporated.
5. Spread the dough evenly onto a jelly roll pan and brush the top of the dough with the egg white and remaining 2 tablespoons of sugar.
6. Sprinkle with nuts or fruit if desired.
7. Bake until golden brown, approximately 25 minutes.
8. Cool for a short time, then cut, while still warm, into bar shapes.

A NEW YEAR

When President Obama spoke with Oprah Winfrey for a "Christmas at the White House" special, he gave himself a "good, solid B+" for his first 11 months in office.

Mrs. Obama was not asked to rate her performance but she might well have given herself an "A" for the garden, a triumph in its maiden year. "This has been one of the greatest things that I've done in my life so far," she had told the crowd at the opening of the new farmers' market near the White House.

So far, so good, and many people cheered a First Lady apparently more eager to get her hands dirty to bring fresh vegetables to the national table than to choose new china patterns.

Still, as the year and the decade turned, what kinds of self-improvements did Mrs. Obama pledge? She resolved, we know, to make it her mission to combat childhood obesity along with promoting good eating habits. She dubbed her 2010 campaign "Let's Move," and invited top athletes to tape TV spots emphasizing the twin role of exuberant physical activity in juvenile health. The new initiative was bound to make the inflatable "Moon Bounce" that had graced the White House lawn back in October seem like, well, kids play.

It remains to be seen how far gardening as a national priority will go into the new decade. Will Americans continue to take up their hoes and purchase seed packets? Will Mrs. Obama get bored with gardening and try other things?

The initial appeal of the Obamas growing vegetables had been enormous. In the first year of the White House Kitchen Garden, 43 million U.S. households also planted vegetables, up nearly 20 percent from the year before, according to the National Gardening Association. Seed sales zoomed up and up.

THE CHEF GAMES OF FALL/WINTER

The autumn White House garden was the stealth-star of an "Iron Chef America" episode that aired on the Food Network on January 3. The show opened with the contestants on the White House south portico. Home team chef Cristeta Comerford partnered with Bobby Flay. Opposing them were Mario Batali and Emeril Lagasse.

The challenge: To make five dishes within an hour, showcasing the kitchen garden's bounty. Michelle Obama instructed them: "Take as much of it as you need."

Cut to the knights of cookery pillaging the garden, then to Kitchen Stadium in New York. Due to the lag between picking and taping, nearly identical vegetables stood in for the Washington ones, but the jars of honey came from the White House. Ready, set go. The chefs raced around, cracking eggs, rolling dough, chopping vegetables, and checking the clock.

Lagasse-Batali came up with caramelized scallops with fennel and white icicle radishes; an oyster and salad trio; sweet potato ravioli; fried turkey and honey-marinated quail; and carrot beignets (doughnuts) with Creole coffee.

Comerford-Flay produced fennel and apple salad with oysters; fried lobster and squid in carrot juice on a plate with sweet and sour eggplant, pine nuts and currants; broccoli clam chowder; and a barbecue pork dish with slaw, collard-green tamales, cauliflower gratin and watermelon radish pickles. For dessert, they offered a version of pie— sweet potato, of course, with honey-pecan brittle and ginger ice cream.

And the winners were Comerford-Flay, perhaps because veggies were more central to their menu, which was the point. From the winners:

CAULIFLOWER

The florets on cauliflower, also called curds, are actually flowers in the bud stage. Since this vegetable is related to cabbage, it gives off a strong odor as it cooks, but its flavor is mild.

1 large head cauliflower (about 3 pounds)
2 tablespoons butter
2 tablespoons flour
11/4 cups milk
Kosher salt and freshly ground black pepper, to taste
1/4 teaspoon grated nutmeg
2 cups shredded Gruyere cheese
1/2 cup shredded parmesan cheese
1/4 cup panko (Japanese breadcrumbs) or coarsely ground fresh bread crumbs

1. Preheat the oven to 350 degrees. Spray a 1-quart casserole dish with cooking spray. Trim the cauliflower and cut into florets.

2. Steam the cauliflower in a large pot with a little water over medium-low heat until tender. Remove the cauliflower from the pot and place it on a towel to remove excess moisture.

3. In a medium (2-quart) saucepan, heat the butter over medium heat. When the butter has melted, whisk in the flour. Cook, stirring, for 2 minutes. Add the milk, whisking constantly to make sure there are no lumps. Cook another 3 to 4 minutes, allowing the sauce to thicken. Season with salt and pepper and add the nutmeg.

4. Put the cauliflower into the prepared pan. Top with half of the cheese. Pour the white sauce (bechamel) over the cheese. Top with the remaining cheese and the bread crumbs.

5. Bake, uncovered for 20 to 30 minutes until golden and bubbly.

Serves 6

BROCCOLI

George H. W. Bush hated this vegetable, but you might have a better experience if you grow it yourself and harvest it before the stalks become tough.

This is basically broccoli soup with a clam garnish, which means you can make your own variations. If you don't eat shellfish, use fish or chicken stock in the soup, and garnish it with small chunks of firm white fish, such as cod. Use vegetable stock, and make it a vegetarian soup with a potato and tomato garnish, topped with a sprinkle of chopped herbs.

Tip: If you opt to use clams in the following recipe, steam them first thing so you have clam juice for the chowder.

Chowder:
6 garlic cloves
4 shallots
1 leek, white part only
1 small onion
2 heads of broccoli
1 stalk lemongrass
1 tablespoon butter
1 sprig of thyme
8 cups clam juice or chicken or fish or vegetable stock (or substitute bottled clam juice)
1 bay leaf
Salt and pepper, to taste

Garnish:
2 tablespoons olive oil
6 fingerling potatoes, sliced
1 bunch broccoli rabe
Salt and pepper, to taste
36 clams, steamed (optional)
16 grape tomatoes, sliced in half

For the soup:
1. Slice the garlic cloves, shallots, leek, and onion. Wash the broccoli, slice the stems, and reserve the green florets for the puree. Smash the lemongrass stalk to release its flavor.

2. In a medium saucepan, melt the butter. Add the garlic, shallots, leek, onion and thyme and sauté until fragrant. Add the broccoli stem slices and sauté until the broccoli is softened.

3. Pour in the stock, bay leaf, and lemon grass stalk. Simmer for about 20 minutes.

4. In the meantime, fill a pot with water, sprinkle in some salt, and bring it to a boil. Set a bowl of ice water next to the stove. Add the broccoli florets and blanch for 1 minute. Remove the broccoli florets with tongs or a slotted spoon, and immediately plunge them in the ice water. Drain, purée the broccoli florets in a blender, and set it aside in a bowl.

5. Remove the lemon grass from the soup. In the same blender, spoon in the soup and vegetables and purée the mixture, working in batches if it doesn't all fit at once.

6. Strain the soup through a fine sieve or strainer set over a bowl, pushing with the back of a spoon to help it go through. Stir in the green broccoli-floret purée and season the soup with salt and pepper. Set it aside.

For the garnish:

1. In a sauté pan, heat the olive oil. Add the potatoes and cook until they begin to soften.

2. Add the broccoli rabe and sauté until softened. Season with salt and pepper.

3. Add the tomatoes and clams (optional) and continue sautéing until heated through. Spoon the vegetables and clams into a soup plate or bowl and pour the broccoli soup around.

Makes 1 12-inch pie

The sweet potato plays a starring role in pies, but 19th century botanist George Washinton Carver came up with 100 things to make from it, including flour, lemon drops, and 8 different dyes.

Crust:
1 cup butter
1/2 cup sugar
2 1/2 cups flour
1 teaspoon salt
1 teaspoon vanilla
1 teaspoon lemon zest
2 egg yolks

Filling:
3 sweet potatoes
4 sticks cinnamon
5 star anise
1 orange
2 tablespoons melted butter

Custard:
3 cups crème fraiche (a French-style specialty cream)
4 eggs
1 tablespoon vanilla
2 teaspoons ground cinnamon
1/2 teaspoon ground nutmeg
1/2 teaspoon salt

Honey Meringue Topping:
2 cups honey
3 egg whites

For the crust:

1. In a bowl, using an electric mixer, beat the butter and sugar until light and fluffy.

2. Add the flour and salt; mix gently on low speed.

3. Add the vanilla, lemon zest and egg yolks, beating to incorporate.

4. With your clean hands, form the mixture into a ball, wrap it tightly in plastic wrap, and let it rest in the refrigerator for 30 minutes.

5. With a lightly floured rolling pin on a lightly floured work surface, roll the dough out into a circle approximately 13 inches in diameter and ¼-inch thick.

6. Lightly drape the dough over a 12-inch tart or pie pan. Fit the dough into the pan and trim any remaining dough. Cover the crust with parchment paper and let rest in the refrigerator for another 30 minutes.

7. Preheat the oven to 350 degrees.

8. Place baking beads, dry beans or rice on top of the parchment paper to keep the crust from bubbling as it bakes (this is called blind baking). Bake for 12 minutes. Carefully remove the parchment paper and baking beads.

For the filling:

1. Wash each sweet potato and cut it in half lengthwise. Cut the orange into four equal pieces. Place the sweet potatoes, cinnamon, star anise and orange on a baking sheet and drizzle the melted butter over everything.

2. Bake at 350 degrees until the sweet potatoes are tender (the time will depend on the size of the potatoes).

3. Scoop out the potatoes and discard the skin. Press the potatoes through a sieve or strainer so they turn into a potato purée. Discard the spices and orange. Set the potato purée aside to cool.

For the custard:

1. In a bowl, using an electric mixer, mix the custard ingredients until blended.

2. Add the custard to the potato purée and mix until fully blended. Pour this mixture into the cooked tart shell and finish baking at 300 degrees until set, about 35 minutes.

For the topping:

1. Place the honey in a saucepan. Bring the honey to a boil, then let it simmer over low heat until the liquid is reduced to 1 cup.

2. In a bowl, using an electric mixer, whip the egg whites until stiff.

3. Beat in the hot honey.

4. Spoon this mixture over the cooked sweet potato pie and broil until the meringue browns to a toasted color.

PRESIDENTS DAY

The White House winter garden, protected from the worst of the elements, stayed green in February despite the "Snowmageddon" blizzard that hit Washington early in the month. The First Family's Presidents Day gift to the nation, and most particularly, to Martha Stewart, was the loan of two cooks for a pre-taped Presidents Day show. On Monday, February 15, 2010, White House chefs Cristeta Comerford and Bill Yosses appeared on "The Martha Stewart Show" to demonstrate White House winter recipes

During the taping, Comerford suggested that since Sasha and Malia would not have school on the day that the birthdays of George Washington and Abraham Lincoln jointly are observed, they might spend time helping her cook. Host and guests chatted as they cooked at a flag-decorated table in the TV studio/kitchen.

Stewart teased Comerford about keeping the First Family trim with portion control, but sought confirmation of Barack Obama's pie love from Yosses. The pastry master conceded that the Commander in Chief would go for a cherry pie if one were to be baked, but on the Martha Stewart Presidents Day show it was not.

Instead, the segment featured Comerford's lasagna, said to be an Obama family favorite, which uses winter garden-fresh spinach, and fresh ground turkey (not really late Thanksgiving leftovers). Comerford's salad recipe took advantage of greens from the winter garden, plus honey from First Family bees. For dessert, Yosses whipped up a yogurt-glazed cake loaded with fresh oranges and honey, to be served with baked-apple slices.

Bill Yosses' desserts have been cheering up First Families since George and Laura Bush lived in the White House. He is pictured here with a pan of baked apples, part of an elaborate but relatively healthy Presidents Day dessert.

Serves 6 ———————————————

4 cloves garlic
1 tablespoon olive oil
1 cup chopped yellow onion
1 pound fresh ground turkey
1 (28-ounce) can plum
   tomatoes, crushed
1 (6-ounce) can tomato paste
Salt and freshly-ground black
   pepper, to taste
1 tablespoon chopped fresh
   basil
1 tablespoon chopped fresh
   flat-leaf parsley
15 ounces low-fat ricotta or
   low-fat cottage cheese
3/4 cup freshly grated
         parmesan cheese
1 large egg, beaten
2 pounds fresh spinach
16 cooked lasagna
   noodles
1 pound low-fat
   shredded mozzarella
   cheese

Executive White House Chef
Cristeta Comerford mixes it up
on The Martha Stewart Show.

1. Preheat the oven to 400 degrees.

2. Peel and mince the garlic.

3. In a large skillet, heat the olive oil over medium heat. Add the onion and cook until the onion turns from white to translucently clear. Add the garlic and cook for 1 minute more. Add the ground turkey and cook for about 10 minutes.

4. Add the crushed tomatoes and tomato paste to the turkey mixture, and stir to combine. Season with salt and pepper.

5. Reduce the heat and let the mixture simmer until thickened, about 20 minutes. Stir in the basil and parsley. Remove from the heat and set aside.

6. In a medium bowl, combine the ricotta or cottage cheese, ½ cup of the parmesan cheese, and the egg. Season to taste with salt and pepper.

7. Wash but do not dry the spinach. Place it in a large skillet over medium heat. Cook, stirring occasionally, until wilted. Remove from the heat and set aside.

8 . In a 9-by-13-inch baking dish, ladle 1/4 of the turkey mixture. Spread it so it covers the bottom of the pan. Lay four of the lasagna noodles on top, then add a layer of 1/3 of the mozzarella cheese, followed by 1/3 of the ricotta mixture, 1/3 of the spinach, and another 1/4 of the turkey mixture. Repeat the layers of noodles, mozzarella, ricotta, spinach and turkey two more times. Top with the remaining four noodles. Sprinkle the remaining 1/4 cup of parmesan cheese over the top. Place in the oven and bake until bubbly, 25 to 30 minutes. Let stand about 5 minutes before cutting and serving.

Serves 6

Spiced Walnuts:
1 cup walnut halves
1/2 cup confectioners'
  sugar
1 teaspoon Cajun
  spice mix (available
  at supermarkets)

**White House Honey-
Apple Cider Vinaigrette:**
1 shallot
1/2 cup honey
1/4 cup apple cider
  vinegar
Juice of 1 lemon
3/4 cup extra-virgin
  olive oil
Salt and freshly-
  ground black
  pepper, to taste

Salad:
1 pound mixed winter greens,
  such as chicory, frisee, tatsoi,
  spinach, or arugula
1/2 fresh fennel bulb
1 Granny Smith apple,
  julienned
1 cup spiced walnuts
Salt and freshly-ground
  black pepper, to taste

For the spiced walnuts:
1. Heat a medium skillet over medium heat. Add the walnuts and toast, stirring frequently, until fragrant, about 5 minutes. Be careful not to let them burn.
2. Add the confectioners' sugar and cook, tossing the nuts, until the sugar is melted. Sprinkle with the Cajun spice and toss again. Remove from the heat and let cool.

For the vinaigrette:
1. Peel and mince the shallot.
2. In a small bowl, whisk together the honey, vinegar, lemon juice, and shallot.
3. Slowly whisk in the olive oil. Season to taste with salt and pepper.

For the salad:

1. Wash and dry the greens. Tear any large leaves into bite-sized pieces. Wash the fennel. Using a sharp knife, cut the fennel crosswise (parallel to the stem end) into thin slices. Wash and core the apple. Cut it into thin (julienne) strips.

2. Place the greens, fennel, apple, and spiced walnuts in a large bowl. Add 1/2 cup of the vinaigrette and toss to combine. Season to taste with salt and pepper and toss again before serving. Leftover dressing should be covered, refrigerated and used within a few days.

Cake:

Unsalted butter, as need-
ed for the baking pan
1 large navel orange, cut
into 8 wedges
1 1/2 cups flour
1 1/2 cups sugar
1 teaspoon baking
powder
1/8 teaspoon baking soda
Pinch of coarse salt
1/2 cup plain whole
milk yogurt
1 teaspoon grated
orange zest
1 large egg
3 tablespoons honey
1/2 teaspoon pure
(not imitation)
vanilla extract
1/4 cup freshly squeezed
lemon juice
1/4 cup confectioners'
sugar

Baked apples:

4 red apples, such as
Macoun or McIntosh
2 tablespoons unsalted
butter
1/4 cup honey
1 whole vanilla bean,
scraped
2 tablespoons golden
raisins

For the cake:

1. Preheat the oven to 350
degrees. Grease an 8-by-2-inch
round cake pan with butter. Cut
a circle of parchment paper to fit
the bottom of the pan. Line the
pan with the parchment paper
and grease the parchment paper
with butter.

2. In a medium saucepan, bring
4 cups of water to a boil. Cut
the orange into 8 wedges and remove the seeds. Add the orange
to the water and boil for 5 minutes. Drain the water. Refill the
saucepan with another 4 cups of
water and bring it to a boil. Add
the orange wedges and boil again
for 5 minutes.

3. While the orange is boiling, in a medium bowl, whisk
together the flour, 1/2 cup of the
sugar, the baking powder, baking
soda, and salt.

4. Using a slotted spoon or
tongs, carefully remove the
orange wedges from the boiling water and place them in a
bowl. Add the remaining 1 cup
of sugar to the boiling water.
Cook, stirring until the sugar
is dissolved. Return the orange
wedges to the boiling water

and cook until softened, about 5 minutes. Drain the water in a colander in the sink.

5. Place the orange wedges in the bowl of a food processor, along with, ¼ cup of the yogurt, the orange zest, egg, honey and vanilla. Process until well combined. Add the flour mixture and process again until combined.

6. Transfer the batter to the prepared cake pan. Place in the oven and bake until golden brown and a cake tester inserted into the center of the cake comes out clean, 25 to 30 minutes.

7. While the cake is baking, in a small saucepan, whisk together the lemon juice, confectioners' sugar, and remaining ¼ cup of yogurt. Bring to a boil over medium high heat. Let boil until glaze is thickened, about 3 minutes.

8. Place a wire rack on top of a sheet of parchment paper. Remove the cake from the oven and flip over the pan so the cake comes out onto the rack. Remove the parchment paper round from the top. Pour the glaze over the cake. Let it stand until the glaze is absorbed. Place on a serving plate and serve with sliced baked apples.

For the apples:

1. Preheat the oven to 350 degrees. Using a sharp knife, cut into the stem end of each apple to remove the core, but do not cut all the way through the apple. Its shape should be left intact.

2. In each of 4 jumbo-size muffin pan cups, evenly divide the butter, honey, and vanilla bean seeds. Place an apple in each prepared muffin pan cup. Stuff each apple with about 1 1/2 teaspoons of raisins.

3. Cover each of the apples with a sheet of parchment paper, then place a sheet of aluminum foil on top. Scrunch the foil to secure it around the apple.

4. Bake until the apples are tender, 25 to 30 minutes. Spoon the juices over the apples before serving.

WINTER INTO SPRING

It was time for any gardener to think about what had worked out really well and what had not, and why. It was time to consider changes or additions.

Many gardeners ask themselves and consult with others to determine what they might do to enrich their soil or safely limit weeds or otherwise increase yields. Gardeners who love to cook read up on staggering plantings of their favorite ingredients so more may be enjoyed ripe, and some think upon how to preserve the coming abundance they will not be able immediately to use.

On tables in farm kitchens, suburban dinettes or fancy "great rooms," even in apartment "living areas," seed catalogs pile up, along with snipped-out recipes and new lifestyle DVDs or books. On grey days, computer screens light up with new garden and cooking ideas.

In the White House, the season was also one for assessment of what the garden had accomplished and what might yet be done, and what continuing the garden might mean for the country.

In a sense, the planting of the White House Kitchen Garden had brought us full circle from the days when George Washington dreamed that America would become a "granary for the world" through wheat cultivation. We achieved that long ago but also have learned that being a global breadbasket is not synonymous with security. A focus on the garden in 2010 seemed like a wise choice to help keep Americans grounded.

Cultivating community gardens or our own may diminish our stress, and perhaps our food expenses, while it helps make ourselves and our families more fit.

IT WAS A TIME TO THINK.

ACKNOWLEDGEMENTS

The White House Kitchen Garden inspired this book, but for ideas about bringing children and families into gardens, I turned to community and school gardening programs throughout the country. I am indebted to all of the groups that shared their enthusiasm about gardening with children, keeping my in-box filled with recipes and photos. For invaluable help in providing me with an overview of children's gardening, and connecting me with many of the contributors to this book, I thank Nicci Cagan, Debra Eschmeyer, Emily Jackson, Rose Hayden-Smith, Sarah Pounders, and Michelle Markesteyn Ratcliffe.

Thanks are also due to my agent, Clare Pelino of Pro Literary Consultants. She put me in touch with Ilene Barth of Red Rock Press, who championed this project, suggested to her by food writer Sylvia Carter whom I've never met but also thank. Ilene and the Red Rock Press team shepherded this manuscript with enthusiasm and care.

For professional support and camaraderie, I could always count on my colleagues at the Chautauqua Writers' Center and Grub Street, Inc., as well as the Ladies Who Lunch: Carolyn Faye Fox, Andrea Pyenson, Lisë Stern, Rachel Travers, Cathy Walthers and Lisa Zwirn. For baking advice and last-minute recipe tests, I thank Esther Muhlfelder. For stress relief, I would gladly run another 1000 miles with the Crying Shames, then cool down with the CLG or the Mid-Life Crisis Group.

I also thank my mother, Ann, for patiently listening to constant updates about the book. My husband, George, and children, Jordan and Martha, indulged me as I tested recipes for every vegetable imaginable. Their love and humor helped see me through.

RESOURCES FOR FAMILIES WHO WANT TO GARDEN

Center for Ecoliteracy, www.ecoliteracy.org- supports educational programs for sustainable living.

Farm to School, www.farmtoschool.org - connects schools (K-12) and local farms.

Kids Gardening, www.kidsgardening.org - extensive gardening resources for children, families and teachers, part of the National Gardening Association

Kitchen Gardeners International (KGI), www.kitchengardeners.org – promotes kitchen gardening and sustainable food.

Obamafoodorama, http://obamafoodorama.blogspot.com - a fun ongoing blog about food at the White House

TheWhoFarm, www.whofarm.org - promotes organic gardening on the road and through a blog.

United States Department of Agriculture People's Garden, www.usda.gov - demonstration garden projects at the USDA and information for home gardeners

CONTRIBUTORS

Agape Youth Garden
 Life Changers Family Community
 Lanham, MD

Appalachian Sustainable Agriculture Project
 Asheville, NC   www.asapconnections.org

Carolyn Blount Brodersen
 Ventura, CA   www.whateye8.com

Blue Earth Farms, Chehalis, WA
 www.blueearthfarms.org

Boise Urban Garden School, Boise, ID
 www.boiseurbangardenschool.org

Brainfood, Washington, DC
 www.brain-food.org

Camden Children's Garden   Camden, NJ
 www.camdenchildrensgarden.org

CitySprouts, Cambridge, MA
 http://citysprouts.org

Cleveland Botanical Garden Green Corps
 www.cbgarden.org

Columbus Elementary School, Columbus, NM

Community Design Center of Minn. Garden Corps
 Saint Paul, MN   www.comdesignctrmn.org

Ann Cooper, Boulder, CO
 www.lunchlessons.org

Denver Urban Gardens, Denver, CO
 www.dug.org

Early Sprouts, Keene, NH
 www.earlysprouts.org

Edible Schoolyard, Berkeley, CA
 www.edibleschoolyard.org

From the Ground Up, Stone Ridge, NY
 http://fromthegroundup.us

Gaining Ground, Concord MA
 www.gainingground.org

Garden of the World, Multi-Cultural Center
 Sioux Falls, SD, www.multi-culturalcenter.org

Global Gardens Rosa Parks Summer Program
 Tulsa, OK   www.global-gardens.org

Melissa Graham, Purple Asparagus, Chicago, IL
 www.purpleasparagus.com

Grow Pittsburgh, Edible Schoolyard Program
 Pittsburgh, PA   www.growpittsburgh.org

Kids Can Grow
 U. of New Hampshire Coop Extension
 Dover, NH   http://extension.unh.edu

KIPP McDonogh 15 School for the Creative Arts
 New Orleans, LA

Charles Loomis, Greenlife Grocery
 Asheville, NC and Chattanooga, TN
 www.greenlifegrocery.com

Maha Farm, Clinton Valley, WA
 www.mahafarm.com

Judith Marquez, Columbus, NM

Laurey Masterson, Asheville, NC
 www.laureysyum.com

Mary Lin Elementary School, Atlanta, GA

Mount Vernon Ladies' Association
 www.mountvernon.org

Natick Community Organic Farm,
 Natick, MA   www.natickfarm.org

New York Botanical Garden
 Ruth Rea Howell Family Garden
 Bronx, NY   www.nybg.org

Oakland Based Urban Gardens (OBUGS)
 Oakland, CA   www.obugs.org

Tusculum View Elementary School
 Greeneville, TN, www.ruralsources.net

School Garden Project of Lane County
 Eugene, OR   http://www.efn.org/~sgp

Seeds of Nutrition, Atlanta, GA
 www.mendezfoundation.net

Noah Sheetz, Albany, NY

Joanna Sooper, Milwaukie, OR

Sustainable Food Center
 Austin, TX
 www.sustainablefoodcenter.org

Tiger Post After School Program
 Tiger Post Community Education Center
 Ipswich, SD

Tricycle Gardens/ Neighborhood Resource Cen.
 Children's Learning Garden, Richmond, VA
 http://tricyclegardens.org

Michael Turback   www.icecreamsundae.com

Urban Sprouts, San Francisco, CA
 www.urbansprouts.org

Liz Van Brunt, Chautauqua, NY & Frederick, MD

Rebecca Wheeler, Chicago, IL
 www.rebeccawheeler.com

Wonderland Avenue School
 Los Angeles, CA

Index